Reality Rewritten:
Manifest the Life You Actually Want

By:

Nova Vale

Table of Contents:

Preface

In a world overflowing with information, "manifestation" has become a buzzword, often reduced to glittery Instagram quotes or wishful thinking disguised as advice. But manifestation is far more than that. It's not magic. It's not fantasy. It's a *real* and *tangible* process of reshaping your life by reshaping the way you think, feel, and act.

This book was born out of a desire to bridge the gap between ancient wisdom, modern psychology, and practical, day-to-day application. It's for those who are skeptical but curious. For those who've tried manifestation and felt disappointed. And for those who *know* there's something more to life but can't quite grasp how to reach it.

What makes this book different is its grounding. It doesn't ask you to suspend your logic. It doesn't demand blind faith. Instead, it gives you tools: psychological insights, mindset shifts, real-world examples, and actionable techniques to help you *experience* change rather than just hope for it.

Every technique inside has either worked for me personally, for clients I've guided, or for readers who took that first leap of faith and kept going. It's structured to walk with you step by step: from building a solid mindset foundation to applying the most effective tools available today, including those adapted to our modern lives.

This is more than just a guide. It's a blueprint.

Whether you're seeking more love, wealth, purpose, health, or simply peace of mind, you'll find something here that clicks. Something that feels less like learning something new, and more like remembering what you always knew deep down: that you are the author of your life story.

Let's begin.

Chapter 1: Introduction to Manifestation

- What is Manifestation?
- The Science and Psychology Behind It (simplified)
- Common Misconceptions Debunked

What is Manifestation?

Manifestation is the process of bringing your thoughts, desires, and intentions into your physical reality. In its simplest form, manifestation is about turning ideas and dreams into real-life experiences. It's about aligning your mindset, emotions, and actions with the outcomes you wish to create, and watching those outcomes unfold in your life.

People often associate manifestation with mystical or "magical" practices, but at its core, it is rooted in something much more practical and universal: the power of focus and intention. What you focus on consistently tends to grow. What you believe, you begin to act upon. What you act upon, you often create.

Think of manifestation as planting a seed in a garden. Your thoughts are the seed. Your emotions are the water. Your actions are the sunlight. Over time, with the right environment and attention, the seed grows into something tangible, whether it's a goal achieved, a relationship improved, or a dream realized.

Beyond Wishing: The Active Nature of Manifestation

One of the biggest misunderstandings about manifestation is that it's just about wishing or dreaming. People imagine that if they simply think about something hard enough, it will appear. While positive thinking is a piece of the puzzle, manifestation is much more dynamic.

It involves:

> - Clarity: *Knowing exactly what you want.*
> - Belief: *Trusting that it's possible for you.*
> - Emotion: *Feeling the joy or gratitude as if it's already yours.*
> - Action: *Taking steps in alignment with your desire.*
> - Openness: *Being willing to receive in unexpected ways.*

It's not about controlling every detail of how something happens.
It's about aligning yourself with the outcome you desire and
allowing the process to unfold.

Everyone is Manifesting, All the Time

Here's a powerful truth: whether you're aware of it or not, you're already manifesting every day. The thoughts you repeat, the beliefs you hold, the emotions you live in, and the actions you take, they're all creating your reality in each moment.

If you constantly focus on lack, struggle, or failure, you tend to experience more of the same. But when you intentionally choose thoughts of possibility, gratitude, and abundance, your experiences often shift in that direction too. Manifestation gives you the tools to take conscious control over what you're creating.

Manifestation is Not One-Size-Fits-All

Everyone manifests differently. Some people are more visual; others feel things deeply; some need logical steps while others thrive on creative flow. The goal of this book is to guide you toward discovering your personal style of manifestation. There's no single right way, only the way that works for you.

Why Manifestation Matters Today

In today's fast-paced, often overwhelming world, learning how to manifest consciously can be life-changing. It reconnects you with your inner power. It helps you move from survival mode into creation mode. It gives you a sense of purpose and direction, rather than just reacting to life as it comes.

When you learn to manifest with clarity and confidence, you stop waiting for change to happen. You start creating it.

The Science and Psychology Behind It (Simplified)

Manifestation may sound mystical, but much of its power is rooted in science, particularly in how the brain works, how emotions influence behavior, and how our perceptions shape reality. Let's break it down into simple, practical explanations that help you understand why manifestation *actually works*.

The Reticular Activating System (RAS): Your Brain's Filter

Your brain is constantly bombarded with information, millions of pieces of data every second. But you can only consciously process a tiny fraction of it. That's where the Reticular Activating System (RAS) comes in. It acts like a mental filter, helping you notice what's important to you.

Here's the key:
Your RAS pays attention to what you focus on.

If you keep thinking, "I'm always broke," your RAS will highlight everything that supports that idea: unpaid bills, rejections, lack. But if you focus on abundance, opportunity, or growth, your RAS starts noticing things like job openings, creative ideas, and people who can help you.

This is why affirmations, visualization, and goal setting are so effective. They train your brain to look for and act on what you desire.

Neuroplasticity: Rewiring Your Brain

Neuroplasticity is your brain's ability to change, adapt, and grow. When you think a thought repeatedly, you strengthen the neural pathways associated with it. Over time, these pathways become habits - mental and emotional "defaults."

Manifestation uses this concept by helping you:

> ➢ Replace limiting beliefs with empowering ones
> ➢ Build confidence through repetition
> ➢ Create a new mental "normal" that aligns with your goals

Example:
If you start affirming, "I attract opportunities easily," and take small actions in line with that belief, your brain begins to accept it as reality, and you'll naturally start behaving in ways that support it.

Mirror Neurons and Emotional Contagion

When you observe someone experiencing something: joy, success, love - your brain lights up in similar ways as if *you* were experiencing it. These are called mirror neurons, and they help explain how visualization works.

When you visualize a desired outcome and feel the emotions tied to it (like excitement, peace, or confidence), your brain starts to "believe" it's happening. That belief influences how you act, speak, and respond, creating real change in your outer world.

The Self-Fulfilling Prophecy Effect

The self-fulfilling prophecy is a psychological phenomenon where your expectations influence your behavior, which in turn influences outcomes.

For example:

> ➢ If you believe you'll succeed, you tend to try harder, stay optimistic, and recover faster from setbacks – that's leading to actual success.
> ➢ If you believe you'll fail, you may give up easily, avoid risks, or miss opportunities – that's leading to failure.

Manifestation trains you to set intentional expectations that guide your subconscious behaviors toward success.

Emotion as Fuel: The Role of Feelings in Creation

Your emotions are powerful signals that shape your actions and decisions. Positive emotions like joy, gratitude, or love put your body in a state of openness and energy, while negative emotions like fear or doubt create resistance and hesitation.

When you align your emotions with your goals - feeling as though what you want is already real - you become a magnet for opportunities and solutions.

This is why manifestation often emphasizes:

> ➢ Feeling "as if" you already have it
> ➢ Practicing gratitude now, not just later
> ➢ Shifting emotional states before taking action

Why Manifestation Has a Scientific Basis

➢ Your brain focuses on what you repeat (RAS).

➢ Your thoughts reshape your mental wiring (neuroplasticity).

➢ Your emotions and imagination influence real behavior (mirror neurons).

➢ Your beliefs shape your outcomes (self-fulfilling prophecy).

➢ Your emotional state fuels your energy and decisions.

So while manifestation may feel magical, much of its effectiveness is grounded in how your mind and body already function. You're not creating something *out of nothing*. You're learning to guide your brain, energy, and actions in a way that brings what you desire into reality.

Common Misconceptions Debunked

Manifestation has become a buzzword in recent years, and with that popularity comes a lot of confusion. From social media soundbites to misunderstood advice, many people approach manifestation with unrealistic expectations or misconceptions that actually *block* their progress. Let's clear those up.

Misconception #1: "Manifestation is Just Wishing and Waiting"

Truth:
Manifestation isn't magic, and it's not passive. It's a process that combines your thoughts, emotions, and actions. You can't just think about something and wait for it to land in your lap, you need to participate in the process.

You still need to:

- ➢ Take aligned action
- ➢ Recognize opportunities
- ➢ Stay emotionally and mentally engaged

Think of it like ordering a package online. You place the order (intent), but the delivery system (universe + action) needs your address, confirmation, and sometimes even a signature (effort).

Misconception #2: "You Have to Be Positive 100% of the Time"

Truth:
This is one of the most harmful myths. Nobody is positive all the time, and forcing positivity can actually suppress real emotions - which creates internal resistance.

You don't manifest through perfection. You manifest through authentic   alignment.
It's okay to feel fear, doubt, or sadness. The key is learning to process those emotions and shift your focus gently, without guilt.

Progress comes from:

> Self-awareness
> Emotional honesty
> A consistent return to your intention, not constant cheerfulness

Misconception #3: "If It Hasn't Manifested Yet, Something's Wrong with Me"

Truth:
This belief creates shame and pressure, and it's simply not true. Timing, alignment, readiness, and even growth behind the scenes all play roles in manifestation.

Sometimes:

> You're being prepared emotionally or mentally
> Better opportunities are on their way
> You're being protected from something that doesn't serve your long-term good

You're not broken. You're just evolving.

Misconception #4: "Manifestation Means Never Struggling Again"

Truth:
Manifestation isn't a ticket to a perfect, struggle-free life. Challenges still come, but you'll approach them differently. You'll have more tools, more trust, and more creative power to shape how you respond and move forward.

Think of manifestation as building a strong foundation. Life may still bring storms, but you'll know how to navigate them with purpose and power.

Misconception #5: "You Can Manifest Anything Instantly"

Truth:
While some manifestations can appear quickly, most take time, alignment, and consistent effort. Instant manifestation is rare and often depends on how closely your desire aligns with your beliefs and current vibration.

The timeline varies depending on:

- ➢ Your internal blocks or beliefs
- ➢ How emotionally invested you are
- ➢ Whether you're taking aligned action
- ➢ Whether it truly serves your greater good

Patience and trust are part of the process.

Misconception #6: "You're 100% in Control of Everything That Happens"

Truth:

This one is subtle but important. While you do have creative power, you're not *in control* of every external detail. Manifestation is a co-creation between you and the universe (or life, or your subconscious - however you define it).

You set the direction.

You fuel it with energy.

You act in alignment.

And then you let go of *how* and *when* it arrives.

This creates space for unexpected blessings, creative detours, and divine timing.

Let Go of the Myths. Embrace the Real Power

When you remove the pressure to be perfect, to manifest overnight, or to control every detail, manifestation becomes lighter, more joyful, and more effective. It's not about doing everything "right." It's about showing up consistently with intention, trust, and openness.

The truth is, manifestation isn't reserved for the lucky or the spiritual elite. It's a natural process that anyone can learn, and you're already on the path.

Chapter 2: Setting the Foundation

- The Power of Belief and Mindset
- How Thoughts Shape Reality (With Simple Analogies)
- Understanding Energy, Frequency, and Vibration (Non-Woo Explanation)
- Emotions as Amplifiers: Why Feeling is the Secret Ingredient

The Power of Belief and Mindset

If manifestation is the engine that drives your dreams forward, then belief and mindset are the fuel. Without them, even the most well-planned goals stall. With them, even the most impossible visions start to feel achievable.

Before we dive into more techniques, it's critical to understand just how powerful your beliefs and mindset truly are, and how they shape everything you manifest.

What You Believe, You Begin to Experience

At its core, a belief is simply a thought you've repeated so often that you accept it as truth. Once a belief is formed, your brain and behavior start working to make it *real*. That belief acts like a filter through which you interpret the world.

If you believe:

> ➤ "I'm unlucky," you'll interpret neutral events as bad signs.
> ➤ "I'm not good enough," you'll hesitate to try new things or sabotage opportunities.
> ➤ "Good things are always coming to me," you'll stay open and confident, even when things look uncertain.

Your beliefs shape your decisions. Your decisions shape your reality.

Mindset: The Silent Sculptor of Your Life

While beliefs are the specific thoughts you hold, your mindset is the general *attitude* or *framework* through which you operate. It determines how you:

- ➢ React to failure
- ➢ Approach goals
- ➢ Handle change
- ➢ View yourself and the world

There are two main types of mindset:

- ➢ Fixed mindset: Believes abilities and circumstances are set in stone. ("I can't change.")
- ➢ Growth mindset: Believes you can learn, adapt, and create change. ("I can figure this out.")

Manifestation thrives in a growth mindset. It allows you to believe that transformation is possible, even when the outside world hasn't caught up yet.

Why Beliefs Are Often Hidden, and How to Spot Them

The tricky thing about beliefs is that many of them are subconscious. They come from early life experiences, societal messages, or past failures, and they often run quietly in the background.

Some signs you may have limiting beliefs:

> ➢ You procrastinate even though you really want something
> ➢ You feel like you're "not ready" or "not worthy" yet
> ➢ You downplay your desires as "too much" or "unrealistic"
> ➢ You feel excited about a goal but secretly doubt it'll happen for *you*

To shift your beliefs, start by noticing them. Journaling, meditation, and self-reflection can help bring them to the surface.

The Belief Loop: How Your Mind Reinforces Itself

Here's a simple but powerful model:

Belief → Thought → Emotion → Action → Result → Reinforced Belief

If you believe money is hard to make, you'll think thoughts that reflect scarcity, feel stress about finances, take hesitant actions (or none at all) and likely see disappointing results... which then reinforce your belief.

But when you change the belief at the root, the entire cycle changes.

New belief: "Abundance is always available."
That leads to confident thoughts, feelings of trust, bold actions, and better results.

Upgrading Your Belief System

You don't have to completely rewire your mind overnight. Start small:

1. Notice what beliefs you're currently running.

2. Question whether they're true, or just familiar.

3. Replace them with more empowering beliefs.

4. Reinforce the new beliefs through repetition, affirmation, and evidence.

Example:
Old belief: "I'm not good with relationships."
New belief: "I'm learning how to have healthy, loving connections."

Your Mind is Your Magic

Manifestation doesn't start with the outside world. It starts inside, with the stories you tell yourself, the expectations you hold, and the mindset you live in each day. The most powerful thing you can do is believe in your ability to create change.

The mind is not just a tool - it's the sculptor of your entire experience. And when you choose beliefs and a mindset that support your highest vision, manifestation becomes not only possible, but inevitable.

How Thoughts Shape Reality (With Simple Analogies)

You've probably heard the phrase "your thoughts create your reality." But what does that *really* mean? Are we saying that just thinking something makes it happen? Not quite.

What we *are* saying is this:
Your consistent thoughts influence how you feel, how you act, how others respond to you, and what you notice in the world. Over time, this shapes your experiences - often in profound ways.

Let's break this down using a few easy-to-understand analogies. ↓

1. The Mental GPS: Where Your Focus Goes, You Go

Imagine your thoughts are like entering a destination into a GPS. If you keep telling the GPS "I don't want to get lost" or "I don't want to go to the wrong place," it doesn't help much. But when you input a *clear, positive direction* like "123 Success Street," the system guides you there.

Your mind works the same way.

If you constantly focus on what you *don't* want:

> ➢ "I hope I don't mess this up."
> ➢ "I can't afford that."
> ➢ "People always hurt me."

Your thoughts are still guiding you, just in the direction of what you fear or dislike.

But if you focus on what you *do* want:

> ➢ "I'm learning and growing every day."
> ➢ "Money flows to me in many ways."
> ➢ "I attract kind, supportive people."

Then your internal GPS shifts and your choices, emotions, and awareness begin moving you toward that destination.

2. The Thought Garden: You Reap What You Plant

Think of your mind like a garden.

- ➢ Your thoughts are the seeds.
- ➢ Your emotions are the water.
- ➢ Your actions are the sunlight.

If you plant seeds of fear, doubt, or negativity, and tend to them regularly, you'll eventually grow weeds: chaos, confusion, and struggle.

But if you plant seeds of hope, possibility, and trust, and nurture them daily, you'll grow a garden full of opportunities, peace, and abundance.

You can't plant thorns and expect roses. What you consistently think and feel becomes the environment in which your life grows.

3. The Movie Projector: Your Inner World Projects onto the Outer

Picture this: Your mind is a movie projector, and your thoughts are the film reel. Whatever is playing inside gets projected outward onto the screen of your life.

> ➤ If your internal reel is full of doubt, fear, and lack - you'll see those themes show up in your experiences.

> ➤ If your reel is playing confidence, creativity, and worthiness - you'll find yourself acting differently, seeing new opportunities, and attracting better outcomes.

Your thoughts *color your perception* of every event. And your perception affects your reaction, which affects the outcome.

4. The Social Mirror: People Respond to Your Vibe

Have you ever walked into a room where someone is in a terrible mood and you immediately felt the tension? Or met someone so upbeat and positive that you felt energized just being near them?

That's the power of your internal state.

Your thoughts affect your:

> Tone of voice
> Body language
> Energy level
> Decision-making

And other people pick up on that, often without realizing it. This is why confident, self-assured people tend to "attract" success, it's not just luck. It's the result of the energy and mindset they project into the world.

5. The Echo Chamber: What You Put Out Comes Back

Your reality is like a canyon. Whatever you shout into it, it echoes back to you.

- Shout "I'm never good enough," and you'll notice people, situations, and inner thoughts that seem to confirm it.
- Shout "I have value," and soon you'll start hearing that echoed back - from friends, opportunities, and inner strength.

This is often called the *Law of Reflection*: the world mirrors back the energy and beliefs you consistently hold.

Your Thoughts are the Blueprint

> ➤ They influence your emotions.

> ➤ They guide your behavior.

> ➤ They shape your interactions.

> ➤ They color your interpretation of events.

> ➤ They create momentum: either toward success or struggle.

Manifestation starts with thought, but it doesn't end there.

The more you become aware of your thought patterns, the more you can begin choosing them deliberately. Like changing the channel on a TV, you can decide what mental frequency you want to broadcast, and what kind of life you want to receive in return.

Understanding Energy, Frequency, and Vibration (Non-Woo Explanation)

Words like "energy," "frequency," and "vibration" can sound mystical or vague, especially when thrown around without explanation. But there's actually a grounded, science-friendly way to understand them that makes manifestation much more practical and less "woo-woo."

In simple terms, *you are energy*, and so is everything around you.

Everything is Made of Energy

At the atomic level, everything in the universe is made up of atoms, and atoms are mostly empty space, buzzing with protons, neutrons, and electrons. These particles are constantly moving and vibrating.

That includes:

- ➤ Your body
- ➤ Your thoughts
- ➤ Your emotions
- ➤ The chair you're sitting on
- ➤ The phone or screen you're reading this from

This movement and interaction of energy is what gives everything its form, behavior, and even influence.

So when we say someone has "good energy," we're actually describing something real - an observable combination of their body language, emotional tone, presence, and yes, even biological signals like heart rate and breath patterns.

Frequency: The Speed of Vibration

Frequency refers to how fast something vibrates. Think of it like the pitch of a musical note.

> ➢ A high frequency = faster vibration
> ➢ A low frequency = slower vibration

Different emotions have different vibrational frequencies. For example:

> ➢ Joy, gratitude, love = higher frequencies
> ➢ Fear, shame, anger = lower frequencies

This doesn't mean one is "good" and the other "bad" - both are part of the human experience. But the frequency you're operating from affects:

> ➢ The choices you make
> ➢ The opportunities you notice
> ➢ The way people respond to you

In essence: *your frequency influences what you attract and how you experience the world.*

How This Relates to Manifestation

When you think a thought, your brain emits electrical signals - literal energy.

When you feel an emotion, it changes your heart rate, breathing, and chemistry - again, measurable energy.

These mental and emotional states affect your *behavior*, which leads to real-world results. And over time, your baseline frequency shapes your habits, environment, relationships, and goals.

Manifestation works because:

1. Your energy affects how you think, act, and engage with life.
2. Like energy attracts like outcomes (via perception, action, and feedback loops).
3. When your inner frequency matches the reality you desire, you're more likely to see it, pursue it, and receive it.

Simple Analogy: The Radio Station

Imagine your goal is like a song playing on a certain radio station. To hear that song, you need to tune into the right frequency.

If you're tuned into doubt, fear, or frustration, you're on a different station, and the "music" of confidence, clarity, and success won't come through clearly.

But when you raise your internal frequency through focus, belief, action, and emotion, you align with the "station" where your desired reality already exists. That's when you start picking up synchronicities, ideas, connections, and results.

Energy Isn't Woo. It's Reality

You don't have to believe in crystals, chakras, or spiritual guides to understand manifestation. Just look at:

> - How someone's energy can light up a room - or drain it
> - How your mood changes the kind of day you have
> - How your body feels heavier or lighter based on your emotional state
> - How being around certain people uplifts or unsettles you

That's all energy. That's all vibration.
And learning to become aware of your own energy is one of the most empowering tools for creating the life you want.

Emotions as Amplifiers: Why Feeling is the Secret Ingredient

If thoughts are the blueprints of manifestation, then emotions are the electricity that brings those blueprints to life.

Most people think manifestation is all about what you *think*. But here's the truth:

Your emotions are what give your thoughts power.

You can say an affirmation 100 times a day, but if it feels flat, doubtful, or forced, it won't do much. But if you say it once and genuinely *feel* it deep in your gut, it activates your nervous system, shifts your energy, and starts rewiring your brain and behavior.

Emotions Are Energy in Motion

Let's look at the word "emotion" for what it really is:
E-motion = Energy in Motion.

Emotions move you. They change your posture, your expression, your decisions, and your tone of voice. They are the *vibrational signals* your body and mind send out into the world.

That's why emotion can make the difference between:

> ➢ Walking into a room confidently... or shrinking back.
> ➢ Following through on a goal... or quitting early.
> ➢ Trusting your dream... or talking yourself out of it.

The more you *feel* aligned with your goal - excited, proud, grateful - the more magnetic your energy becomes.

Think of Emotion Like Volume Control

Imagine your thought is a song playing on a speaker.

> ➢ If the emotion behind it is low, it's like playing that song at volume 1: you can barely hear it.
> ➢ But if the emotion is strong and genuine, it's like turning the volume up to 10: the whole room feels it.

That's why feeling matters. It turns your thoughts into *loud, clear signals* that shape your body language, decisions, energy, and focus.

The Emotion-Frequency Connection

Earlier, we talked about frequency. Here's how emotions fit in:

Emotion	Frequency Level	Effect on Manifestation
Joy & Gratitude	High	Accelerates attraction, aligns quickly
Hope & Optimism	Moderate-High	Creates momentum and opportunity
Doubt & Worry	Low	Slows things down, causes resistance
Shame & Fear	Very Low	Blocks progress, reinforces lack

High-frequency emotions magnetize the outcomes you want because they put your whole system - mind, body, and behavior - into alignment with abundance and success.

How to Activate Emotion in Your Manifestation Practice

You don't have to "force" happiness all day. But you *can* learn to activate emotion deliberately during manifestation rituals. Here's how:

1. Visualization with Feeling
    Don't just *see* the goal - *feel* it. Imagine holding the keys to your new home. Imagine the relief of paying off your debt. Imagine hugging someone after reaching your dream. Let it move you.

2. Gratitude as a Shortcut
    Gratitude instantly raises your emotional frequency. Start your day or your manifestation work by appreciating what you already have, even the smallest things.

3. Use Music, Movement, and Memory
    o   Listen to a song that lifts your mood.
    o   Dance, walk, or stretch to shift your energy.
    o   Recall a time you felt unstoppable.
        Your body remembers. Use it to generate emotion on command.

It's Not About Fake Positivity. It's About Emotional Intention

You don't have to pretend everything's perfect.
Real emotion is more powerful than forced positivity.

The key is to intentionally feel emotions that support what you want to create, even if only for a few minutes a day. This consistent emotional alignment adds momentum to your manifestation efforts.

Emotion Makes It Real

Thoughts might start the process, but emotions give your intentions life.

- ➢ They amplify your energy.
- ➢ They change your chemistry.
- ➢ They drive your behavior.
- ➢ They signal the universe (and yourself) that you're serious.

When you learn how to *feel as if it's already yours* before it shows up, you shorten the distance between desire and reality.

Chapter 3: Clarity is Key

- Defining Your Desires Clearly
- The Difference Between Wanting and Deciding
- The Role of Specificity vs. Flexibility
- Vision Boards and Journaling: Are They Necessary?

Defining Your Desires Clearly

One of the biggest reasons people struggle with manifestation is this:

They don't actually know what they want.

They think they do.

They say things like:

> ➤ "I want more money."
> ➤ "I want to be happy."
> ➤ "I want a better job."

But these statements are vague. And the universe, like a GPS, needs *specific coordinates* to deliver what you're asking for. If your desires are unclear, the results will be scattered, inconsistent, or delayed.

Why Clarity is Crucial

Clarity creates focus. Focus creates direction. Direction creates momentum.

Without clarity:

> ➢ Your thoughts are scattered.
> ➢ Your emotions get mixed.
> ➢ Your actions become unfocused.
> ➢ Your results are hit-or-miss.

Think of manifestation like ordering from a restaurant. If you just say, "I want food," the waiter won't know what to bring. But if you say, "I want the grilled salmon with lemon garlic sauce," the order is clear - and the kitchen gets to work.

Three Keys to Defining Your Desires

Here's how to start making your desires clear, strong, and specific:

1. Get Specific, but Stay Open

Clarity isn't about controlling every detail. It's about knowing the *essence* of what you want.

> ➤ Instead of "I want more money," say:
>   "I want to earn $5,000 a month doing work I enjoy."
> ➤ Instead of "I want love," try:
>   "I want a deeply connected relationship where I feel valued, supported, and inspired."

Then, stay open to *how* it happens.
Be specific in the *what*, flexible in the *how*.

2. Use the 5Ws Technique

Ask yourself these questions to refine your vision:

> ➤ What do I truly want?
> ➤ Why do I want it?
> ➤ Who is involved or impacted?
> ➤ Where does this take place?
> ➤ When do I want this to happen (or begin)?

These questions turn a fuzzy goal into a vivid picture your mind and energy can actually work with.

3. Feel into the Details

Once you've defined your desire clearly, ask:

> ➢ How will I feel when I have it?
> ➢ What will a day in that reality look like?
> ➢ What kind of person would I become to live that version of life?

When your mind can "see" it and your heart can "feel" it, you've given your subconscious and the universe a clear, emotional blueprint to follow.

Avoid the Trap of 'Shoulds'

When defining your desires, don't chase what you think you *should* want.

> ➤ Not what your family expects.

> ➤ Not what society glamorizes.

> ➤ Not what everyone else is doing.

Get honest about what you want: what makes you feel alive, fulfilled, and aligned. Authenticity is powerful fuel in manifestation. When your desire comes from within - not external pressure - it gains clarity and magnetism.

Tools to Help You Gain Clarity

Here are a few simple practices to help define your desires:

> *Journaling Prompts:*
> "What would my ideal day look like?"
> "If I could wave a magic wand and have one thing right now, what would it be?"
> "What am I craving emotionally, not just physically?"
> *Mind Mapping:*
> Draw your main desire in a circle, then branch off with related ideas: emotions, people, outcomes, locations, etc.
> *Vision Board or Mood Board:*
> Images and words help your mind create a clearer inner picture of what you're aiming for.

Clarity Activates Power

The clearer your desires, the easier it becomes to:

> Focus your thoughts
> Align your emotions
> Take meaningful action
> Recognize opportunities
> Signal your intention to the universe

Manifestation doesn't start with wishing. It starts with knowing what you want, and owning it with confidence and intention.

The Difference Between Wanting and Deciding

Most people say they *want* things:

> ➤ "I want to be rich."
> ➤ "I want to be healthier."
> ➤ "I want to be in love."

But wanting alone rarely changes anything. That's because wanting is passive - it leaves the door open to "maybe," "someday," or "if everything lines up just right."

Deciding, on the other hand, is an energetic commitment. It's active.
It says:
"This is happening. I'm making it real."

Wanting is Wishing, Deciding is Claiming

Imagine you're standing at a buffet table.

> ➤ Wanting is looking at the food and saying, "That looks good. I'd love to have that."
> ➤ Deciding is putting the food on your plate and walking away with it.

One is passive observation. The other is aligned action.

The universe responds much more strongly to energy that's committed, clear, and certain. That's what a decision does - it sends a bold, unmistakable signal.

The Power Shift That Happens When You Decide

Here's what changes when you stop wanting and start deciding:

When You Want...	When You Decide...
You stay in "waiting" mode	You shift into "creation" mode
You doubt whether you're ready	You act as if you already are
You overthink or hesitate	You take steps, even if small
You chase after signs	You become the sign
You feel powerless	You reclaim your power

When you decide, you claim your role as the creator, not the observer. You stop hoping and start *becoming*.

What Deciding Actually Looks Like

Deciding doesn't mean knowing *every* step or controlling the outcome.

It means:

> ➤ Locking in your vision
> ➤ Committing to move toward it, no matter what
> ➤ Refusing to entertain the idea of failure
> ➤ Aligning your identity with the version of you who already has it

For example:

> ➤ Saying, "I want to write a book someday" keeps it optional.
> ➤ Saying, "I've decided I'm writing a book this year, even if I don't know how yet" moves the universe (and your subconscious) into action.

The Energetic Signature of a Decision

When you *decide*, your thoughts, emotions, and behaviors begin to organize themselves around your goal, often in subtle but powerful ways:

> ➢ You notice different opportunities.

> ➢ You feel more connected to your goal.

> ➢ You become more resilient.

> ➢ You naturally make choices that support your vision.

That inner shift - from maybe to must - is when true manifestation begins.

How to Practice Deciding

1. *Write a "Declaration List"*
   Instead of "I want" statements, write a list of "I have decided" declarations. Example:

   - o "I've decided to live in alignment with joy."

   - o "I've decided to attract supportive, uplifting relationships."

   - o "I've decided to build a career that lights me up."

2. *Speak it with Certainty*
   Say it aloud. Look in the mirror. Feel it. You're not *hoping* anymore, you're committing.

3. *Back It With Micro-Actions*
   Decisions become real through action. Take even one small step that reflects your decision - today.

Decide and It's Done

Wanting is the seed.

But *deciding is when you plant it, water it, and claim it as yours.*

Once you've truly decided, the world begins to reorient around your intention. That's when manifestation stops being a fantasy and starts becoming your new reality.

The Role of Specificity vs. Flexibility

When it comes to manifestation, there's a sweet spot between being *crystal clear* and staying *open to magic*.
This balance is called: Specificity with Flexibility.

Be specific about what you want.
Be flexible about how it arrives.

Many people either:

> ➤ Get *too vague*, so nothing sticks, or

> ➤ Get *too rigid*, so they block better options they didn't see coming.

Let's break this down.

Why Specificity Matters

Specificity gives your subconscious mind a clear target. It sets your reticular activating system (the part of the brain that filters attention) to start spotting opportunities related to your goal.

When you're specific, you:

> ➢ Focus your energy and emotion
> ➢ Take more aligned actions
> ➢ Notice chances you'd otherwise miss
> ➢ Strengthen belief in the reality of your desire

Example
Instead of saying, "I want a better job," say:
"I want a fully remote job where I earn $80K+, feel appreciated, and have time for my family."

Now your brain knows what to look for. The universe can work with that.

But Don't Get Attached to the 'How'

Here's the key: *Don't micromanage the path.*

When you're too attached to *how* your desire must unfold, you limit what's possible.

You might think the only way to earn money is through a certain job, but the universe might be trying to deliver it through a side project, a new client, or even a random opportunity you haven't imagined.

The "how" is not your job.
Your job is to stay aligned, open, and ready.

Flexibility Keeps You in Flow

Flexibility doesn't mean being indecisive. It means being *receptive*. You still hold a strong vision, but you stay curious about how it might arrive.

- You might manifest the relationship you want, but not with the person you originally thought.
- You might get the income goal you set, but through a totally unexpected channel.

Often, what we want comes better than expected if we allow room for it.

Analogy: Ordering at a Restaurant

Think of it like ordering food:

- Specificity is telling the waiter: "I'd like the grilled chicken with lemon, no dairy, side of rice."
- Flexibility is being okay if the rice is brown rice instead of white, or if they surprise you with an extra sauce.

You're not just saying "bring me food" (too vague), and you're not demanding one exact outcome down to the molecule (too rigid). You're clear, but open.

How to Practice Both

1. *Set a Clear Intention*
   Define what you want in detail. Write it out. Visualize it.
   Feel it. Give your subconscious a picture to hold onto.

2. *Detach from the Outcome's Form*
   Don't obsess over timelines, specific people, or step-by-step
   scenarios. Let life surprise you.

3. *Ask for "This or Something Better"*
   When visualizing or affirming, end with:
   "This, or something better, now manifests for me."
   This tells the universe you're open to aligned upgrades.

4. *Stay Present and Watch for Nudges*
   Stay tuned to intuitive hits, signs, and shifts in direction.
   Your higher self might guide you in ways your logical mind
   wouldn't expect.

Balance Is Everything

Specificity gives your desire direction.
Flexibility gives it wings.

When you find this balance, manifestation becomes less about control and more about co-creation.

You stay clear but open. Focused but trusting.
That's when the *real magic* happens.

Vision Boards and Journaling: Are They Necessary?

If you've ever explored manifestation, you've probably heard about vision boards and journaling. They're often portrayed as "must-do" tools for success. But are they really *necessary*?

The short answer is:
No, they're not mandatory. But when used correctly, they can be powerful tools.

Let's explore what they actually do, why they work (when they do), and how to use them effectively, *without turning them into a chore*.

What is a Vision Board, Really?

A vision board is a collection of images, words, or symbols that visually represent your goals, desires, or ideal life.

The idea is:

> ➤ When you *see* something often, you begin to *believe* it.
> ➤ When you believe it, you start aligning your thoughts, emotions, and actions with it.
> ➤ That alignment speeds up manifestation.

"What you focus on, expands."

It's not the board itself that has power. It's what it does to your focus, energy, and belief system.

What Journaling Really Does

Journaling is another form of intentional clarity. When you write out your thoughts, desires, or plans, it helps:

> Organize your mental clutter
> Deepen your emotional connection to your goals
> Reinforce belief through repetition
> Identify blocks, limiting beliefs, or patterns

There are different styles of manifestation journaling, including:

> Scripting: *Writing in present-tense as if your desire already happened*
> Gratitude Journaling: *Noticing what's already working to raise your vibration*
> Affirmation Writing: *Repeating empowering beliefs to rewire the subconscious*
> Emotional Dumping: *Releasing doubts or fears to clear space for alignment*

Do You *Need* These Tools to Manifest?

Not at all.
Manifestation is about clarity, belief, and alignment - not supplies or routines.

Some people manifest powerfully just by visualizing in their mind. Others thrive with structured tools.

Vision boards and journaling are just that: tools. Not requirements. If they work for you, amazing. If they don't feel aligned, skip them. What matters is how they make you feel.

If they make you feel inspired, use them.
If they make you feel pressured or drained, let them go.

How to Make Them Work for You

If you choose to use vision boards or journaling, keep these tips in mind:

1. Focus on Feeling, Not Just Images or Words

It's not about cutting out pretty pictures, it's about *emotionally connecting* to them. When you look at your board or journal, ask:

> ➤ Does this excite me?
> ➤ Does it feel real or possible?
> ➤ Does it reflect *who I'm becoming*?

2. Quality Over Quantity

A board with 3 strong, emotionally charged goals is better than one cluttered with 50 random desires. Same with journaling - consistency beats perfection.

3. Keep It Visible and Enjoyable

Put your board where you'll see it daily. Let journaling be a calming or energizing ritual, not a box to check.

4. Update as You Grow

Your desires evolve, and so should your tools. Refresh your board or style of journaling as your clarity deepens.

Use What Resonates

Vision boards and journaling are *helpful*, not *mandatory*. They're like glasses for your inner vision: if they help you see better, wear them. If not, find what works for you.

The core principles of manifestation don't change:

- ➢ Clarity
- ➢ Belief
- ➢ Emotion
- ➢ Aligned action

If vision boards or journaling help fuel those, they're absolutely worth it.
If not, trust that your mind, heart, and intention are enough.

Chapter 4: Techniques That Actually Work

- Visualization 2.0: Adding Emotion and Senses
- The "Wouldn't It Be Nice If..." Technique
- Scripting with a Twist: Writing Future Diary Entries
- The 17-Second Rule (Abraham-Hicks inspired)
- The Two-Cup Method (for beginners and skeptics)
- The "Quantum Shift" Meditation for Beginners

Visualization 2.0: Adding Emotion and Senses

Visualization is often seen as simply "picturing what you want." But to truly make it effective and transformative, you need to go deeper.

Welcome to Visualization 2.0:
A practice where you don't just *see* your desires… you *feel*, *hear*, *smell*, and *embody* them.

Why Regular Visualization Falls Flat

Most people visualize like they're watching a movie:
Detached. Passive. Surface-level.

This can work to an extent, but it lacks power. The subconscious mind doesn't respond to words or vague images - it responds to emotion, sensory input, and repetition.

To make your mind believe your desired reality is *already real*, you have to feed it the same kind of input it gets from real experiences. That means:

- Emotions
- Sights
- Sounds
- Touch
- Smells

The more *real* it feels, the more effectively your subconscious (and the quantum field) begins to align with it.

How to Practice Visualization 2.0

1. Get into a Calm, Receptive State

Before visualizing, quiet your mind. A few deep breaths, a short meditation, or even soft music can help shift you into a relaxed, suggestible state.

2. Pick One Scene, Not a Montage

Instead of flipping through desires like a highlight reel, pick one powerful scene - as if you're stepping into a moment from your future life.

Examples:

> ➢ Waking up in your dream home
> ➢ Holding the published version of your book
> ➢ Hugging a loved one after good news
> ➢ Seeing the notification of your first $10K month

Make it vivid, but focused.

3. Engage All Your Senses

Ask yourself:

> ➢ What do I see around me? Colors? Shapes?
> ➢ What do I hear? Voices? Nature? Applause?
> ➢ What do I feel on my skin? Warmth? Soft fabric?
> ➢ What do I smell in the air? Coffee? Ocean breeze?
> ➢ What do I taste if you're eating or celebrating?

You don't have to force all of them, just include whatever feels natural.

4. Most Important: Feel the Emotion

What would you be feeling if this moment were happening *right now*?

> ➢ Relief?
> ➢ Joy?
> ➢ Pride?
> ➢ Peace?
> ➢ Gratitude?

Let that emotion rise in your body. Let it fill you. That's the *signal* that activates manifestation.

Your emotions are the frequency you're broadcasting.
The stronger and more consistent the emotion, the clearer the signal.

5. Repeat Daily (But Lightly)

You don't need to do this for hours. Even 2-5 minutes a day is powerful, if it's emotionally rich.

Don't turn it into a chore. Let it feel like *visiting the future you already love.*

Bonus Tip: Use Anchors

You can pair your visualization with a sensory anchor - something physical that reminds your body of that emotion.

Examples:

> ➤ A specific essential oil you sniff while visualizing
> ➤ A hand gesture you repeat when feeling joy
> ➤ A piece of music that transports you into that moment

Over time, your brain begins to associate that anchor with your desired emotion, making it easier to access the feeling on demand.

Make It Real. Now

Visualization isn't just daydreaming.
It's *rehearsing your future in the present.*

By engaging your senses and emotions, you train your mind to accept your desire as familiar - and that's when alignment kicks in.

Don't just see it. *Live it.*
Don't just wish for it. *Feel it now.*

That's Visualization 2.0.

The "Wouldn't It Be Nice If..." Technique

Sometimes, when we try to manifest big desires, we feel pressure. We start thinking things like:

> ➤ "What if it doesn't work?"
> ➤ "How can I make it happen faster?"
> ➤ "This feels too far away."

That pressure creates resistance, and resistance *blocks* manifestation.

This is where the *"Wouldn't It Be Nice If..."* technique comes in. It's simple, light-hearted, and incredibly effective because it bypasses resistance and gently opens the door to possibility.

What Is It?

The technique is exactly what it sounds like:
You start thinking or speaking your desires using the phrase:

"Wouldn't it be nice if..."

Examples:

> ➤ "Wouldn't it be nice if I got a message today that made me smile?"
> ➤ "Wouldn't it be nice if money came in from an unexpected place?"
> ➤ "Wouldn't it be nice if I felt totally confident in my next interview?"
> ➤ "Wouldn't it be nice if everything started working out for me?"

This technique was popularized by Abraham-Hicks and is designed to feel soft, playful, and *non-threatening* to the mind.

Why It Works

1. It Feels Safe

Unlike bold affirmations like "I AM a millionaire," which can trigger internal disbelief, this method sounds more like gentle daydreaming. Your subconscious is more willing to *play along* without resistance.

2. It Opens Your Energy

The phrase carries *hope*, not desperation. It puts you in a receiving mode: curious, open, and relaxed.

3. It Invites Possibility

Instead of "trying to make it happen," you simply explore what could happen. That shift in energy is powerful.

"Wouldn't it be nice if…" is an energetic wink to the universe.

How to Use It

1. Use It When You're Stressed or Stuck

If you're feeling doubtful, anxious, or blocked, switch to this phrase to soften your energy.

Example:
Instead of "I have to make $500 today," try:

"Wouldn't it be nice if I made $500 today doing something fun and easy?"

Feel the difference?

2. Make It a Daily Practice

You can:

> ➢ Say it aloud in the morning
> ➢ Write 5 "Wouldn't it be nice if…" sentences in your journal
> ➢ Use it during a walk or while brushing your teeth

3. Use It in Conversations (When Appropriate)

You can even use this technique subtly in conversations:

"Wouldn't it be nice if this project just fell into place?"

You're planting seeds *without sounding overly woo-woo.*

Follow the Energy

If a "Wouldn't it be nice if..." sentence makes you smile or feel a flicker of excitement, stay with it. Let yourself imagine it a little more. That emotion is the activation point.

The stronger the *feeling*, the faster the *shift*.

Lightness Attracts

You don't need to force or control every outcome.
Sometimes, the most powerful thing you can do is *lighten up*.

"Wouldn't it be nice if..." is a backdoor into alignment. It opens the mind, raises your vibration, and turns heavy wanting into joyful curiosity.

Try it right now:
Wouldn't it be nice if your desires started unfolding faster than you expected?

You're already on your way.

Scripting with a Twist: Writing Future Diary Entries

Scripting is a popular manifestation technique where you write as if your desires have already come true.

But this version - "Future Diary Entries" - adds a twist that makes it feel even more real and emotionally engaging.

Instead of writing a bland list like "I have a new car, I live in a big house…"
You write a diary entry as if it's the *end of your perfect day in the future.*

This not only activates vivid emotions, but it also tricks your subconscious into thinking this life already exists.

Why This Technique Works

When you write about your future like it's *already happened*, your brain starts creating new neural pathways. To your subconscious, a vividly imagined experience is *almost as real* as a physical one.

And here's what that does:

- ➢ Rewires your beliefs ("This is normal for me now.")

- ➢ Aligns your feelings with your desired reality

- ➢ Reduces resistance, because you're not "asking", you're *remembering*

You become the version of yourself who's *already living* the life you want.
And that alignment is the true catalyst for manifestation.

How to Do It: Step-by-Step

1. Pick a Future Date

Choose a date that feels exciting - but not too far away.
It could be a few weeks or months ahead.

Example:

"August 15th, 2025"

2. Set the Scene

Start writing like it's the end of that day, and you're reflecting on everything amazing that happened.

Example Opening:

"Dear Diary,
Wow. Today was incredible. I can't believe how beautifully everything is falling into place…"

3. Be Specific, But Natural

Describe moments with detail, but keep the tone casual, like a real diary entry. Include:

> ➤ Who you were with
> ➤ What you saw or felt
> ➤ What happened that surprised you
> ➤ What you're grateful for

Example:

"I woke up in my new apartment, and the sunlight coming through the big windows felt so warm. I made coffee in the new kitchen. Still can't believe I have granite countertops! I got an email about a podcast invitation, and I felt so proud of how far I've come..."

4. Feel as You Write

The key ingredient is emotion. As you script, let yourself *feel*:

> ➤ Gratitude
> ➤ Excitement
> ➤ Calmness
> ➤ Pride
> ➤ Joy

If you feel even a little emotional shift while writing, you're doing it right.

5. End with Appreciation

Wrap up your entry like you would at the end of a meaningful day.

Example:

"I'm so thankful for everything that's unfolding. I'm finally becoming the version of me I've always dreamed of."

Tips to Maximize Its Effect

> Use handwriting if possible. It helps anchor emotion better than typing.

> Read it back to yourself occasionally, especially before bed.

> Keep all your future entries in one journal to track your evolution.

> Don't overthink or edit, just let it flow.

You can do this once a week, or whenever you want to reconnect with your vision.

Become the Author of Your Reality

Scripting with future diary entries allows you to step into the story of your future self before it arrives.

And as you live and breathe this reality on paper, your energy shifts. Your identity evolves. Your timeline bends.

Don't just write what you want.
Write who you've become.

And then... become it.

The 17-Second Rule (Abraham-Hicks Inspired)

A tiny window, a massive energetic shift.

According to Abraham-Hicks, 17 seconds of pure, focused thought is enough to start the process of manifestation.

At 17 seconds, your thought begins to gather momentum.
At 68 seconds, the energy is strong enough to begin physical creation.

This isn't about how long you can *want* something. It's about how long you can hold a single, emotionally-charged thought without contradicting it.

Why 17 Seconds?

It's not just a random number. Here's the reasoning:

Your vibration activates when you focus on a thought. If you hold that thought purely (with no doubt, worry, or contradiction) for 17 seconds… The Law of Attraction kicks in, and similar thoughts begin to magnetize toward it. This builds energy, emotion, and momentum.

Think of it like lighting a match.
The first few seconds are delicate. Then suddenly: flame.

How to Use the 17-Second Rule

This practice is ultra-simple and can be done anywhere, in less than a minute.

1. Choose a Clear, Positive Thought

Pick something that excites or inspires you.

Examples:

> ➤ "I love the freedom of working from anywhere."
> ➤ "I feel amazing in my dream home."
> ➤ "Money flows to me in fun, unexpected ways."
> ➤ "My body feels strong, healthy, and energized."

Important: The thought must feel *good* to you. If it doesn't, choose a smaller or more believable version.

2. Set a Timer (Optional)

17 seconds may sound short, but in focused thought, it's longer than you think.

You can:

> ➤ Set a 17-second timer on your phone
> ➤ Count slowly in your mind
> ➤ Or use a stopwatch for 68 seconds if you want to go further

3. Focus Fully - No Distractions

Close your eyes.
Hold the thought.
Feel it.
Expand on it naturally in your mind.

Let the energy grow:

"I love this life… it's so peaceful… I'm doing what I love… waking up excited every day… things just work out for me…"

If you go past 17 seconds - great! You're building energy and emotional resonance.

4. Do It Often, Lightly

You can do this:

> ➢ Right after waking up
> ➢ Before bed
> ➢ While showering
> ➢ During a walk
> ➢ Anytime you want to shift your state

It doesn't need to be a big ritual. Just a few clean, undistracted moments of energetic alignment.

What Happens After 68 Seconds?

According to Abraham-Hicks, once you reach 68 seconds of aligned thought, the manifestation process has *truly begun*. It's as if you've launched a rocket of intention, and the universe starts arranging the pieces.

"Holding a pure thought for just over a minute can be more powerful than hours of action taken from a place of doubt."

Common Pitfall: Mixing Thoughts

If you start thinking:

> ➤ "But how will it happen?"
> ➤ "What if it doesn't work?"
> ➤ "Am I doing this right?"

.. then the signal gets muddy.

The goal is purity, not perfection.
So if a contradicting thought shows up, gently let it go and return to the feeling.

17 Seconds to Start Manifesting

Don't underestimate the power of short, focused intention.
The 17-Second Rule is the easiest way to align your energy with
your desires, even when you're busy or low on motivation.

One thought.
Seventeen seconds.
That's all it takes to begin changing your reality.

The Two-Cup Method (For Beginners and Skeptics)

A simple ritual to shift your reality using only water and intention.

The Two-Cup Method became popular through the manifestation and quantum shifting communities for one reason: it's shockingly simple, and surprisingly powerful.

Even if you're a total skeptic, this technique offers a tangible way to "see" your intention shift, by using water as a symbolic and energetic medium.

What Is the Two-Cup Method?

It's a ritual where you use two cups, two pieces of paper (or sticky notes), and water to symbolically shift from your current reality to a desired one.

It draws from principles of:

> ➢ Quantum physics (multiple realities exist simultaneously)
> ➢ Water memory (water absorbs and carries energetic information)
> ➢ Ritual psychology (rituals create belief and focus)

In short, it helps you mentally and energetically "move" from where you are to where you want to be.

How It Works (Step-by-Step)

You'll Need:

- ➢ Two cups or glasses
- ➢ Water (filtered or tap is fine)
- ➢ Two pieces of paper or sticky notes
- ➢ A pen

Step 1: Label Cup One – Your Current Reality

On the first piece of paper, write a short description of something you're experiencing now that you'd like to change.

Examples:

- ➢ "Stuck in a 9-5 I don't enjoy"
- ➢ "Living paycheck to paycheck"
- ➢ "Feeling anxious and overwhelmed"
- ➢ "Single and lonely"

Stick this label onto Cup 1. This represents your current state.

Step 2: Label Cup Two – Your Desired Reality

On the second piece of paper, write what you want to shift into.

Examples:

> ➤ "Doing meaningful work with flexible hours"
> ➤ "Financially free and stable"
> ➤ "Calm, balanced, and joyful"
> ➤ "In a loving, happy relationship"

Stick this onto Cup 2. This represents the new reality you want to enter.

Step 3: Pour the Water

Fill Cup 1 (Current Reality) with water.
Hold it in your hands. Close your eyes.
Take a moment to acknowledge your current situation - not in judgment, but with awareness.

"This is where I am. But I'm ready for change."

Step 4: Shift Your Focus & Intention

Now, pour the water from Cup 1 into Cup 2.

As you pour, imagine yourself shifting realities.
Feel the transition from the old version of you to the new one.

Focus on how it feels to already be living in that desired reality.
Let the act of pouring represent the shift.

Step 5: Drink the Water

Now, drink the water from Cup 2 slowly and intentionally.

As you drink, imagine you are absorbing the energy of your desired life.
Feel it integrating into your body, your cells, your consciousness.

Why It Works

Even if you don't believe in "water memory" or quantum jumping, this method works because it engages:

> ➢ Your mind (through focus and intention)
> ➢ Your body (through ritualized action)
> ➢ Your emotions (through symbolic transformation)

It becomes a physical anchor to a mental and emotional decision. That alone has power.

When to Use This

> ➢ When you feel stuck in a pattern
> ➢ Before a new moon or full moon (optional)
> ➢ When trying to let go of a limiting belief
> ➢ When you need to *feel* a change before you see it

You can repeat the ritual with different focuses or do it once and let it go.

Tips for Best Results

> ➢ Do it in a calm, private space.
> ➢ Use visualization and emotion as you pour and drink.
> ➢ Afterward, act like the shift already happened. Think, speak, and behave as the new version of you.

Belief doesn't have to come first.
Sometimes, action creates belief.

Water as a Portal

The Two-Cup Method is simple.
But it's also symbolic, emotional, and activating. And sometimes, *that's exactly what manifestation needs.*

Don't underestimate small rituals.
They can ripple into your entire reality.

The "Quantum Shift" Meditation for Beginners

Tap into the version of you that already has what you desire.

Quantum shifting isn't about science fiction or parallel universes. It's about aligning your identity and energy with the version of you who already has the life you want.

This guided meditation technique is simple, beginner-friendly, and powerful when practiced consistently. It's about stepping out of your current self and into your "next level" self: consciously, emotionally, and energetically.

What Is a Quantum Shift?

A "quantum shift" is a sudden and dramatic change in your internal state - your beliefs, feelings, and identity - which results in visible external change.

Rather than chasing your desires from the outside-in, you shift who you're being on the inside first.

You're not trying to "get" the thing.
You're becoming the version of you who already has it.

This is the real essence of manifestation: alignment over effort.

Why Meditation Works for This

Meditation creates:

> Stillness, so you can access deeper mental states

> Focus, to clearly feel and embody your new identity

> Emotional resonance, which imprints the new version of you into your subconscious

By meditating into this version of yourself, you bypass resistance and allow your energy to begin *matching* what you want.

The Quantum Shift Meditation: Step-by-Step

You can do this in just 10–15 minutes a day.

Step 1: Get Comfortable and Breathe

Sit or lie down in a quiet space.
Close your eyes. Begin breathing slowly and deeply.
Let go of tension in your body.
With every breath, feel yourself settle into the present moment.

Step 2: Imagine the "Future You"

Now, bring to mind a version of yourself who already:

- Has the thing you want
- Lives the life you desire
- Feels free, confident, aligned, fulfilled

See them in a full scene.
Where are they?
What are they doing?
How do they carry themselves?
How do they feel?

Let the picture become vivid.

Step 3: Step into That Version of You

Here's the shift:

Step into their body.

Imagine merging with them, like putting on a suit or swapping roles in a movie.
You are now *them*.

Feel their:

> ➢ Confidence
> ➢ Calm certainty
> ➢ Energy
> ➢ Thoughts
> ➢ Posture
> ➢ Gratitude

Sit in that identity for a few minutes. Soak it in.

If it feels "unrealistic" or fake, breathe through that. Stay with it anyway. The more you practice, the more natural it becomes.

Step 4: Anchor the Energy

Ask yourself:

- ➢ "How does this version of me speak?"
- ➢ "What decisions do they make?"
- ➢ "What are they no longer tolerating?"
- ➢ "What are they grateful for right now?"

Let emotions rise. Smile if you feel it. Let it become real in your body, even just for this moment.

Step 5: Return Gently

After a few minutes, begin to return to your current awareness, slowly.
Take a deep breath.
Say silently or aloud:

"Thank you. I remember who I am becoming."
Or simply:
"It is done."

Open your eyes when ready.

Do This Daily, Not Desperately

This isn't a magic trick.
It's a practice, a way to realign yourself *every day* with the reality you're creating.

It's about showing your subconscious:

"This is who I am now."

When your internal world consistently holds that energy, your external world catches up, often in surprising ways.

Tips to Make It Stick

- ➤ Use soft music or a guided voice to stay relaxed.
- ➤ Visualize the same future self often - it builds familiarity.
- ➤ Journal right after to capture any insights or emotions.
- ➤ Act like your future self today, even in small ways.

Identity First, Results Second

The Quantum Shift Meditation teaches you this:

You don't attract what you want.
You attract what you are.

So become it: mentally, emotionally, energetically.
And reality will follow.

Chapter 5: Daily Manifestation Habits

- Morning Routines for High-Vibration Days
- Evening Reflection Rituals
- Micro-Affirmations Throughout the Day

Morning Routines for High-Vibration Days

Start your day in alignment, and watch everything else fall into place.

How you begin your morning sets the tone for your energy, focus, and mindset for the entire day. A rushed, scattered start leads to a chaotic frequency. But a conscious, high-vibe morning plants the seeds of manifestation from the moment you open your eyes.

The goal isn't perfection. It's intentionality.

Here's how to create a morning routine that aligns you with your desires, raises your vibration, and grounds you in your manifestation mindset, even if you only have 10 minutes.

Why Mornings Matter

When you first wake up, your brain is in a theta-alpha wave state. This is the same state used in hypnosis - it's when your subconscious is most open to influence.

So instead of grabbing your phone, checking the news, or rehashing yesterday's problems, use this precious window to align your energy with what you want.

Core Elements of a High-Vibration Morning

You don't need to do all of these every day, but even a few can create noticeable shifts:

1. Wake Up with a Gentle Reminder

Keep a positive statement or intention by your bed.

Examples:

- ➤ "Today, I create magic effortlessly."
- ➤ "I am becoming the version of me who already has it."
- ➤ "Everything is always working out for me."

You can write this on a sticky note, keep it in a journal, or say it mentally before getting up.

2. Hydrate and Breathe

Before coffee, drink water - it reactivates your body and energy system.

Then do 3–5 deep breaths to center yourself.

This grounds your nervous system and opens space for intuition.

3. Set Your Energetic Intention

Ask yourself:

> ➢ "How do I want to feel today?"
> ➢ "What energy do I want to carry?"
> ➢ "Who am I becoming today?"

Let your answers guide you. Choose one or two words like:

> ➢ Calm
> ➢ Confident
> ➢ Magnetic
> ➢ Grateful
> ➢ Abundant

Say it aloud or write it down.

4. Visualization in Miniature

Take 1–2 minutes to visualize your day going beautifully:

> ➢ Picture walking into work with ease
> ➢ Imagine a joyful conversation
> ➢ Feel successful, abundant, and aligned

You're not forcing outcomes, you're *pre-aligning your energy*.

5. Movement to Shift State

This could be:

> ➢ A 10-minute yoga flow
> ➢ Dancing to one empowering song
> ➢ A short walk in nature
> ➢ Just stretching with intention

Movement helps shift stagnant energy and anchors your mindset in your body.

6. Gratitude Lightning Round

List 3 things you're grateful for, quickly and from the heart.

Example:

> ➢ "My warm bed"
> ➢ "Clean water"
> ➢ "Opportunity to evolve today"

Gratitude is a frequency amplifier. It opens the door for more to flow in.

A Sample 10-Minute High-Vibe Morning

1. Wake up + say your sticky note affirmation (30 sec)
2. Drink water + deep breathing (1 min)
3. Set energetic intention (1 min)
4. Quick visualization (2 min)
5. Light movement (3 min)
6. Gratitude list (2 min)

Done. You've just programmed your vibration for the day.

Advanced Add-Ons (If You Have More Time)

➤ Journaling future diary entries
➤ Full guided quantum meditation
➤ Reading one page from a manifestation book
➤ Saying mirror affirmations

Tip: Consistency Over Complexity

You don't need a 2-hour ritual.
You just need consistent energetic focus, even 10 minutes a day can completely change your reality over time.

"Win the morning, win the vibration. Win the vibration, manifest the reality."

Evening Reflection Rituals

End your day in alignment to reset your energy and deepen your manifestations.

If mornings are for planting energetic seeds, evenings are for clearing, realigning, and nourishing your vibration before sleep - a time when your subconscious mind does its most powerful work.

Sleep is not just rest, it's integration.

By ending your day with intention, you prime your mind and energy to manifest even while you sleep. Here's how to create a nightly ritual that supports your manifestations, releases emotional residue, and closes your day on a high-frequency note.

Why Evening Rituals Matter

Your last thoughts before bed linger in the subconscious for hours. If you fall asleep in a state of worry, stress, or scarcity, that energy embeds deeper.

But if you fall asleep in gratitude, peace, and alignment, your subconscious mind continues to attract from that space, even in your dreams.

Core Elements of an Evening Manifestation Ritual

You don't need to do all of these every night. Choose what resonates, and make it your own.

1. Gentle Review Without Judgment

Take a moment to ask:

> ➤ "What went well today?"
> ➤ "What made me feel aligned, joyful, or proud?"
> ➤ "Where did I feel resistance and what can I learn from it?"

No guilt. No perfectionism. Just gentle awareness. This builds emotional intelligence, a key to intentional manifestation.

2. Gratitude Rewind

Mentally rewind your day and pick out 3–5 things you're truly grateful for.

Even if your day felt hard, look for the smallest gifts:

> ➤ A kind message
> ➤ A good meal
> ➤ A breath of fresh air
> ➤ Learning something new

Gratitude heals and resets your energy field.

3. Emotional Release or Reset

Don't take emotional clutter to bed with you. Try one of the following:

- ➢ Write out what you're ready to release
- ➢ Do 1–2 minutes of deep belly breathing
- ➢ Imagine your stress dissolving in a stream of golden light
- ➢ Say aloud: "I release all that no longer serves me"

This clears stuck vibrations and makes room for fresh alignment.

4. Future Pacing with Feeling

Now bring your desired reality to mind. Picture it already done: feel the emotions of peace, success, love, or abundance.

As you lay in bed, imagine:

- ➢ Receiving the message you've been waiting for
- ➢ Seeing your bank account growing
- ➢ Holding the hand of a loving partner
- ➢ Waking up in your dream home

This isn't wishing. It's rehearsing your new identity.

5. Sleep Affirmations (Optional)

Repeat one calming affirmation in your mind as you drift off. Some examples:

> ➢ "I am safe, aligned, and worthy."
> ➢ "My desires are already mine."
> ➢ "Everything is working in my favor."
> ➢ "The universe supports me while I sleep."

This becomes your last energetic imprint of the day and sets the tone for tomorrow.

A Sample 10-Minute Evening Ritual

1. Quick journal or mental review (2 min)
2. Gratitude rewind (2 min)
3. Deep breathing or release (2 min)
4. Visualize your future self (3 min)
5. Sleep affirmation (1 min)

Simple. Intentional. Powerful.

The "Reverse Gratitude" Trick

Before sleep, try saying thank you for things you haven't received yet, as if they're already here.

Example:

> ➤ "Thank you for the financial breakthrough."
> ➤ "Thank you for the beautiful opportunity coming my way."
> ➤ "Thank you for the peace I feel every day."

This trains your subconscious to expect your desires, and to act accordingly.

Your Day Ends How You Decide

Ending your day with love, clarity, and intention allows your entire being to rest in alignment. Over time, this nightly ritual becomes a quiet but powerful co-creator.

What you rehearse in the silence of night becomes your reality in the light of day.

Micro-Affirmations Throughout the Day

Small words, big shifts.

Affirmations are powerful. But often, people treat them like long mantras they must repeat 100 times in front of a mirror. That can work, but micro-affirmations are a much more sustainable, everyday approach to aligning your mindset.

They're quick, casual, and quietly powerful. You use them *in the moment, on the go*, and *under your breath*. Done right, they reprogram your subconscious without overwhelming your routine.

What Are Micro-Affirmations?

Micro-affirmations are short, easy-to-remember phrases that:

> - Reframe negative thoughts on the spot
> - Nudge you toward a high-vibe state
> - Interrupt self-sabotage patterns
> - Create momentum without pressure

They're like mental nudges that say:

"Hey, you're still creating. Stay aligned."

Why They Work

Your subconscious mind is always listening. The words you whisper to yourself throughout the day, especially during stress, doubt, or boredom, become your dominant vibration.

Micro-affirmations help redirect your inner dialogue without needing a formal practice.

Think of them as energetic tuning forks.

When to Use Them

➢ Waking up: *"Today is full of good surprises."*
➢ In the shower: *"Abundance flows to me with ease."*
➢ While walking: *"I'm supported. I'm aligned. I'm ready."*
➢ During traffic: *"Delays mean divine timing."*
➢ Before a meeting: *"I radiate calm confidence."*
➢ After a setback: *"Everything is a setup for something better."*
➢ While spending money: *"Money comes back multiplied."*
➢ Before sleep: *"It's safe to let go. My dreams are already on the way."*

Examples of Powerful Micro-Affirmations

Keep these short, sweet, and emotionally believable:

> ➢ *"I've got this."*

> ➢ *"Something amazing is unfolding."*

> ➢ *"It's already working."*

> ➢ *"I choose peace."*

> ➢ *"My energy is magnetic."*

> ➢ *"This moment is enough."*

> ➢ *"I don't chase, I attract."*

> ➢ *"Even this is part of it."*

> ➢ *"Aligned, not rushed."*

> ➢ *"I'm becoming her/him/them."*

Write a few of your own that feel natural to say in your daily rhythm.

How to Make Them Stick

1. Anchor them to daily triggers
   Tie affirmations to habits like brushing your teeth, drinking water, or checking your phone.

2. Keep them visible
   Use sticky notes, lock screens, or journal headers.

3. Use them as emotional redirects
   When you catch yourself spiraling or doubting, drop a micro-affirmation. Shift your story in real time.

4. Say them like you mean it, or whisper them when needed
   Even quiet repetition has power. Intention is what makes them work.

Create a "Vibe Vault"

Keep a note in your phone titled "Affirmations That Work for Me."
Update it often with lines that truly *hit*. Read it like a menu when
you need an energetic reset.

In Short

You don't need loud, dramatic affirmations to shift your reality.
You need *consistent alignment in small doses*, and that's what
micro-affirmations deliver.

What you say casually… eventually becomes your reality
intentionally.

Chapter 6: Shadow Work and Self-Sabotage

- Why You Might Be Blocking Your Own Manifestations
- Healing Limiting Beliefs and Inner Conflicts
- Forgiveness as a Manifestation Accelerator

Why You Might Be Blocking Your Own Manifestations

Sometimes, the only thing standing between you and your desire… is you.

This might be the hardest truth to accept on your manifestation journey:
You're always manifesting, even the things you don't want.

It's not about blame. It's about awareness.

Most people don't get stuck because they're doing manifestation "wrong." They get stuck because there's a *hidden part* of them that doesn't feel ready, safe, or worthy of receiving what they're asking for.

This is where shadow work enters the picture.

What Is Shadow Work?

Shadow work is the process of exploring the unseen parts of yourself, the ones you may have rejected, suppressed, or hidden, usually because they were uncomfortable or painful.

These include:

- ➢ Old wounds
- ➢ Limiting beliefs
- ➢ Unprocessed emotions
- ➢ Protective patterns
- ➢ Subconscious fears

And these "shadows" often drive your energetic signals more than your conscious intentions.

You say you want abundance - but deep down, you fear visibility.
You affirm love - but secretly feel unworthy of it.
You visualize success - but associate it with burnout or betrayal.

Until these hidden parts are seen, acknowledged, and integrated, they'll continue to *block, delay, or distort* your manifestations.

Signs You Might Be Self-Blocking

Here are common clues that your subconscious might be resisting what your conscious mind desires:

> ➢ You *almost* get what you want, then lose it.

> ➢ You feel uncomfortable or anxious about the thing you say you want.

> ➢ You procrastinate, sabotage, or "forget" to take aligned action.

> ➢ You constantly shift desires, never landing on one thing.

> ➢ You feel tension in your body when visualizing your dream outcome.

> ➢ You attract situations that reinforce your old identity.

These aren't signs of failure. They're *feedback loops* from your subconscious.

Why the Subconscious Blocks What You Consciously Want

Your subconscious is not evil or broken. It's trying to protect you.

It's operating off old programming, beliefs, and emotional associations. If you learned, for example, that:

> ➢ Money creates conflict

> ➢ Love leads to abandonment

> ➢ Success brings isolation

> ➢ Attention is dangerous

…then your subconscious will resist those things, even while your conscious mind tries to manifest them.

The inner child doesn't care about your vision board.
They care about feeling safe, loved, and accepted.

The First Step: Radical Self-Honesty

Ask yourself:

> ➤ "What am I afraid will happen *if I actually get what I want*?"

> ➤ "What belief might be blocking this desire from feeling safe?"

> ➤ "What part of me might *not* want this, and why?"

The answers might surprise you, but they're gold.

This isn't self-blame. It's self-reclamation.

Practical Ways to Spot Self-Blocking Patterns

1. Notice emotional resistance:
   Do you feel tight, anxious, or "off" when visualizing your dream life?

2. Watch your language:
   Do you say "I want it" and "I don't deserve it" in the same breath?

3. Track your habits:
   Are your daily actions aligned with your goals, or protecting you from fear?

4. Pay attention to triggers:
   What people, ideas, or opportunities make you react strongly? That's often where your shadow is hiding.

Next Step: Work with the Block, Not Against It

Instead of shaming yourself for these blocks, *get curious* about them. Ask:

> ➤ "What is this part of me afraid of?"
> ➤ "What belief is being activated right now?"
> ➤ "How can I make it safer to receive what I want?"

The moment you acknowledge and validate your resistance, it begins to loosen its grip.

What You Need to Remember

Manifestation isn't about forcing good vibes. It's about creating *congruence* between what you say you want and what your whole self believes, feels, and expects.

You're not broken.
You're layered.
And you can align those layers to become a powerful, conscious creator.

Healing Limiting Beliefs and Inner Conflicts

You can't manifest beyond what you believe is possible for you.

You've probably heard the phrase *"your beliefs shape your reality."* But what does that really mean?

At its core, manifestation is not about *forcing* your desires into existence. It's about becoming an energetic match for them. And your beliefs are the blueprint that determine what you're able to receive.

Limiting beliefs act like invisible walls around your potential. You might have a clear desire, take inspired action, and still feel stuck because somewhere deep down, a part of you doesn't believe it's *safe*, *possible*, or *deserved*.

That's not a failure. That's a signal.

What Are Limiting Beliefs?

Limiting beliefs are stories (usually subconscious) that tell you:

- Who you are

- What you deserve

- What's possible or impossible

- What life "should" look like

They're often formed during childhood, shaped by family, culture, religion, trauma, or repeated emotional experiences. And once they're embedded, they quietly run your thoughts, feelings, actions, and... manifestations.

Common Examples of Limiting Beliefs:

➤ *"I'm not good enough."*

➤ *"Success is for other people, not me."*

➤ *"If I have more, others will have less."*

➤ *"Money is hard to make."*

➤ *"I always mess things up."*

➤ *"Love never lasts."*

➤ *"Good things don't happen to people like me."*

These beliefs act like filters. They twist how you interpret opportunities, risks, compliments, or even miracles. You might manifest a new chance and talk yourself out of it without even realizing why.

What Are Inner Conflicts?

An inner conflict is when two parts of you are pulling in opposite directions.

Example:

> ➢ One part of you wants to be wealthy.

> ➢ Another part is terrified that wealth will make people judge or abandon you.

Result? Manifestation gridlock.

This isn't you being lazy or confused. It's you being *internally split*. And no amount of scripting or visualizing can override that until those parts are reconciled and realigned.

Healing Begins with Awareness

Ask yourself:

> - "What would I have to believe about myself to think I can't have what I want?"

> - "What am I afraid will happen if I succeed?"

> - "Whose voice is this belief really - mine, or someone else's?"

> - "Which part of me is in conflict with this desire, and why?"

This process takes courage, but it opens the doorway to healing.

How to Heal Limiting Beliefs (Step-by-Step)

1. Identify the belief.
   Example: "I'm not worthy of love."
2. Question its truth.
   - "Is this universally true?"
   - "Did I *choose* to believe this, or did I inherit it?"
   - "What evidence challenges this belief?"
3. Find the origin.
   Ask: "When did I first start believing this?" You'll often find a memory, person, or pattern at the root.
4. Replace it with a new, empowering belief.
   Make sure it feels believable to your nervous system.
   - Instead of "I'm lovable," try "I'm learning to see my worth."
5. Reinforce the new belief.
   - Use micro-affirmations
   - Visualize yourself acting from the new belief
   - Surround yourself with people, content, and environments that reflect it

Releasing the Emotional Charge

Sometimes, limiting beliefs are entangled with emotional residue - shame, guilt, grief, fear.

To release that energy:

> ➤ Journal it out (write letters you never send)

> ➤ Cry or move your body

> ➤ Speak it aloud in a safe space

> ➤ Use EFT tapping or breathwork

> ➤ Practice inner child connection and reassurance

The more emotion you move, the lighter your energy becomes, and the easier your new beliefs can anchor in.

Remember: Beliefs Are Not Truths

They're just thoughts you've repeated long enough to feel "real."

And just as they were created, they can be rewritten.

When you heal your beliefs, you shift your point of attraction.
When you resolve your inner conflicts, you unlock energetic flow.
That's when manifestation becomes effortless.

Forgiveness as a Manifestation Accelerator

You can't hold onto the past and walk into your future at the same time.

When people think of manifestation, they usually picture vision boards, affirmations, and high vibes. Forgiveness? Not so much. But here's a powerful truth:

Unforgiveness is a weight.
It anchors you to old energy, and that energy becomes your signal to the Universe.

Whether it's toward someone else, your past, or even yourself, unhealed resentment and regret can slow down (or completely block) your manifestations.

Forgiveness isn't just about morality. It's about energetic freedom.

Why Forgiveness Matters in Manifestation

When you're holding on to pain, betrayal, or shame, you're locked into a frequency of:

> ➤ Lack

> ➤ Fear

> ➤ Self-protection

> ➤ Bitterness

> ➤ Distrust

That frequency *clashes* with the energy of your desires, especially if you're trying to manifest love, abundance, joy, or new beginnings.

Forgiveness doesn't mean you condone what happened.
It means you're choosing to stop replaying the past and start reclaiming your power.

Forgiveness of Others: Freeing Your Flow

Holding onto anger at others keeps you energetically tied to them. You're still letting them shape your emotions. and therefore your point of attraction.

Ask yourself:

> ➤ "How much longer do I want to carry this person in my field?"
> ➤ "Who am I when I'm not defined by this pain?"

Forgiving others is ultimately for you. It doesn't excuse them. It releases you.

Try saying:

"I forgive you not because it was okay, but because I deserve peace."

Forgiving Yourself: The Ultimate Reset

This is the most underestimated block in manifestation - self-blame.

You might unconsciously believe you:

> Ruined your chances
> Don't deserve better
> Can't be trusted to receive more

These inner judgments act like energetic roadblocks. Until you release them, you'll find ways to punish or limit yourself, even while saying you want more.

Self-forgiveness is the bridge between who you've been and who you're becoming.

Affirm to yourself:

"I forgive myself for not knowing what I know now. I'm allowed to grow."

Practical Forgiveness Ritual (5 Minutes Daily)

1. Sit quietly. Close your eyes.
2. Bring someone or something to mind you haven't forgiven (including yourself).
3. Say (out loud or in your mind):

   > "I'm willing to release this pain. I give myself permission to be free."

4. Breathe deeply. Imagine light or warmth dissolving the emotional charge.
5. Say thank you - to the lesson, to yourself, to the process.

You don't have to force it. Willingness is enough to start.

Forgiveness Makes Space

Manifestation is not just about *calling things in.*
It's about clearing space so that what you want has room to arrive.

Forgiveness isn't weakness. It's strength.
It's not forgetting. It's *transcending.*
And when you forgive, you vibrate in a frequency where miracles can find you.

Chapter 7: Inspired Action & Aligned Effort

- How to Recognize Intuitive Nudges
- Letting Go Without Giving Up
- The Magic of Doing Less (The Detachment Principle)

How to Recognize Intuitive Nudges

Inspired action feels light, effortless, and exciting. Forcing outcomes feels heavy, exhausting, and rigid.

One of the most powerful tools in manifestation is inspired action. But how do you know when action is truly inspired versus when it's coming from a place of fear, desperation, or impatience?

Intuitive nudges are the Universe's way of guiding you toward your desires. They're gentle, subtle promptings that align you with the flow of your manifestations. It could be an idea, a feeling, a sudden urge to take action. These nudges come when your energy is in alignment with what you desire.

But here's the key: Intuitive nudges don't come with a sense of urgency. They feel calm, clear, and right.

The Difference Between Intuition and Impulse

Intuitive Nudges:

> - Calm, gentle, clear.
> - They feel aligned with your purpose.
> - They arise spontaneously and are often unexpected.
> - They don't come with pressure.

Impulsive Action:

> - Driven by anxiety or fear.
> - Feels rushed or out of desperation.
> - Often tied to a specific outcome or result.
> - Comes with resistance or doubt.

Signs You're Receiving Intuitive Nudges

1. *You feel drawn to do something without understanding why:*
   Perhaps it's a new project, a place to visit, or a person to reach out to. You simply feel a magnetic pull, even if it doesn't fully make sense at first.
2. *It feels effortless:*
   Inspired action doesn't feel like hard work or a struggle. You feel energized by the task, even if it's a challenge.
3. *You're excited, but calm:*
   There's excitement, but it's not anxiety. There's trust that everything is working out, even if the next step feels a little uncertain.
4. *It aligns with your deeper values and vision:*
   When you're tuned into your intuition, the action you take feels connected to your deeper purpose. It feels like the right thing to do, even if it's not the most obvious or logical step.

How to Strengthen Your Intuition

Quiet your mind:
You can't hear intuitive nudges over the noise of stress, worry, and overthinking. Practice stillness, whether through meditation, journaling, or mindful breathing.

Trust your gut feelings:
Intuition often speaks in physical sensations: a feeling in your stomach, a sudden sense of clarity, or a peaceful knowing. Start paying attention to these signals.

Practice daily mindfulness:
Pay attention to the little nudges you get throughout the day. The more you acknowledge and act on small intuitive calls, the easier it will be to recognize the big ones.

Act without overthinking:
Often, intuition speaks in the present moment. Don't overanalyze or second-guess. Trust that the guidance you receive is aligned with your highest good.

Letting Go Without Giving Up

Once you receive an intuitive nudge to take inspired action, the next step is to let go of the need for control.

Many people think that manifesting requires constant action, effort, and struggle. But sometimes, the most powerful action is to simply let things unfold. This doesn't mean you stop taking inspired action, but you release any attachment to the outcome.

The Paradox of Letting Go

Letting go can feel counterintuitive. How can you manifest your desires if you aren't constantly pushing for them?

Here's the key:
When you let go, you're detaching from fear and doubt. You're trusting the process and allowing the Universe to work behind the scenes. Letting go doesn't mean giving up. It means surrendering to the flow and knowing that everything is coming together perfectly, even if it doesn't look that way at the moment.

Why Letting Go Is So Powerful in Manifestation

It releases resistance:
The more you hold tightly to an outcome, the more resistance you create. Letting go softens the grip on your desires, creating an open space for them to come into your life.

It allows things to come in the right timing:
Manifestation isn't about rushing the process; it's about trusting that what's meant for you will arrive at the right time.

It aligns you with the present moment:
You start to focus on what you can do now, instead of stressing over what you can't control.

The Magic of Doing Less (The Detachment Principle)

Less isn't always less. In fact, sometimes doing less can actually accelerate your manifestations.

This is known as the detachment principle. When you're detached from a specific outcome, you're free to let things unfold naturally, without forcing them into existence. Ironically, this often leads to faster and more powerful manifestations.

How Detachment Creates Space for Your Desires

1. *It frees up emotional energy:*
   When you're attached to the "how" and "when" of your manifestation, you're using energy that could be better spent elsewhere. Detachment allows you to conserve and direct that energy toward feeling good in the present moment.
2. *It invites surprise:*
   Detachment allows the Universe to surprise you in ways you didn't expect. When you release the need for a specific outcome, you open yourself up to greater possibilities.
3. *It invites trust:*
   Trust is a magnet for manifestation. Detachment shows the Universe that you believe in the process, and this belief naturally attracts your desires.

Always Remember

Manifestation isn't about forcing yourself to take endless action or obsessing over outcomes. It's about recognizing when to act with ease and trust, and when to step back and allow things to come to you.

Inspired action flows naturally from clarity and intuition. Letting go isn't giving up; it's creating space for the Universe to work its magic. And doing less can often yield more because it allows you to align with your desires, not your doubts.

The Magic of Doing Less (The Detachment Principle)

Manifestation isn't about doing more. It's about being more aligned.

One of the biggest misconceptions about manifestation is that you have to work non-stop, hustle endlessly, and force outcomes to make things happen.

But manifestation doesn't respond to pressure. It responds to alignment.

The truth is, doing less when rooted in trust and clarity can often lead to more powerful results than frantic over-efforting. This is the heart of the detachment principle.

What Is Detachment in Manifestation?

Detachment means you're not emotionally tied to how or when your desire   shows   up.
You're still focused, you still care, but you're not anxious, desperate, or obsessed.

It's the difference between:

> ➤ *Wanting* something and *needing* it.

> ➤ *Trusting* it will arrive and *demanding* that it happen on your schedule.

You're detached *from the outcome,* but still committed *to the vision.*

Why Less Can Actually Attract More

When you try to control every detail, you send out the signal:

"I don't trust that this is happening unless I push it into place."

But when you let go and lean into ease, you shift into the frequency of:

- ➢ Trust

- ➢ Openness

- ➢ Receptivity

- ➢ Confidence

These are powerful attractors.

And that's when things start to move - often in ways better than you planned.

The Law of Paradoxical Intent

This principle states that the more desperate you are for something, the more you push it away. Why? Because desperation signals lack, and the Universe reflects that back.

When you're calm, grounded, and unattached, you're signaling abundance - the belief that what you want is already yours, or is on the way.

Doing Less Doesn't Mean Doing Nothing

Let's be clear: detachment isn't laziness. It's intentional stillness.

You're not ignoring your goals, you're taking inspired action only when it feels aligned, and not out of panic or pressure.

You're not trying to "make it happen." You're letting it happen.

This includes:

> ➤ Resting when you're tired

> ➤ Saying no to things that don't feel right

> ➤ Trusting your timing

> ➤ Honoring your emotional state

> ➤ Choosing quality over quantity in your actions

How to Practice Detachment

1. *Set your intention clearly*
   Know what you want. Visualize it. Feel it. Then release it
   with confidence.

2. *Focus on your current vibration*
   Shift attention from the outcome to your *state of being.* Ask:
   "How can I feel good today?"

3. *Let go of the 'how' and 'when'*
   Stop micromanaging. Your job is the 'what' and 'why'. The
   Universe handles the rest.

4. *Allow space and stillness*
   Take breaks. Create silence. Allow inspired ideas to flow in
   instead of forcing decisions out.

5. *Affirm your trust*
   Use reminders like:

   > "Things are unfolding perfectly, even if I can't see it
   > yet."
   > "My energy is enough."
   > "The less I chase, the more I attract."

Your Energy Does the Work

Manifestation isn't about how much you do, it's about *who you are while doing it.*

Detachment doesn't mean giving up your desires.
It means you stop fighting against them and *start flowing with them.*

When you let go, you let in.
When you do less with more intention, the Universe fills in the rest.

Chapter 8: Real-Life Applications

- Manifesting Love and Relationships
- Manifesting Money and Abundance
- Manifesting Career and Purpose
- Manifesting Health and Vitality

Manifesting Love and Relationships

Attracting meaningful connections by becoming the energy you seek.

Love is one of the most sought-after areas for manifestation. Whether you're calling in a soulmate, improving an existing relationship, or healing from past heartbreaks - manifesting love starts with *you*.

Many people make the mistake of trying to manifest love from a place of emptiness or neediness. But the truth is, *you don't attract what you want - you attract what you are.*

Become What You Seek

Instead of focusing on "finding" someone, focus on embodying the energy of love.
Ask yourself:

> ➤ How do I want to feel in a relationship?

> ➤ Do I offer that feeling to myself right now?

> ➤ Am I radiating the kind of energy I want to receive?

When you become self-loving, emotionally available, and aligned, you naturally magnetize relationships that mirror that back.

Key Practices for Manifesting Love

1. *Self-Love First*
   - Treat yourself with the same love and respect you desire from a partner.
   - Set healthy boundaries.
   - Take yourself on solo dates.
   - Speak kindly to yourself.
2. *Visualize with Emotion*
   - Don't just imagine a partner, *feel* what it's like to be deeply loved.
   - What does a normal day in that relationship look like?
   - Feel the connection, safety, joy, and passion as if it's happening now.
3. *Release Your Timeline*
   - Desperation pushes love away.
   - Trust that love is on the way and that the timing will be perfect.
   - The more at peace you are with being alone, the more open you are to authentic connection.
4. *Heal Old Stories*
   - If you believe "love is painful" or "I'm not good enough," those beliefs will shape your reality.
   - Use journaling or inner child work to rewrite those narratives.
   - Replace "I always get hurt" with "I attract safe, healthy love."

What to Avoid

- *Fantasizing instead of aligning:* Dreaming about love is great, but if your daily energy is rooted in loneliness, you're sending mixed signals.

- *Over-idealizing a specific person:* Focus on how you want to feel, not who must give you that feeling.

- *Ignoring red flags:* Alignment doesn't mean settling. Trust that the right connection honors your worth.

If You're in a Relationship

Manifestation can also strengthen existing relationships:

- ➤ Visualize improved communication, intimacy, and joy.

- ➤ Appreciate your partner daily - what you focus on grows.

- ➤ Communicate your desires clearly and lovingly.

- ➤ Release control and allow space for your partner to grow.

Affirmations for Love

- ➤ "I am worthy of deep, soulful love."

- ➤ "I attract relationships that nourish and inspire me."

- ➤ "Love flows to me effortlessly and in perfect timing."

- ➤ "I give and receive love freely and abundantly."

So, How to Manifest Love?

Manifesting love isn't about "getting" someone. It's about becoming the version of yourself who already has the love you desire.

That version of you is:

- ➢ Confident

- ➢ Radiant

- ➢ Emotionally open

- ➢ Aligned with the frequency of love

When you live from that space, love can't help but find you.

Manifesting Money and Abundance

Creating financial flow by shifting from lack to alignment.

Money is one of the most emotionally charged topics in manifestation. It can represent freedom, security, power - or fear, struggle, and stress. That's why manifesting money requires more than just desire. It requires energetic alignment.

You don't attract abundance by needing it. You attract it by believing you already live in an abundant universe.

Understanding Your Money Blueprint

Everyone has an internal "money story" shaped by:

- ➤ Childhood experiences
- ➤ Cultural conditioning
- ➤ Emotional associations

If deep down you believe:

- ➤ "Money is hard to come by"
- ➤ "I'm not good with money"
- ➤ "Rich people are greedy"
  Then those beliefs will create energetic resistance, no matter how much you want more income.

To manifest money, you must feel safe receiving it, worthy of having it, and confident handling it.

How to Shift into Abundance Frequency

1. *Heal Your Money Beliefs*
    - Write down every limiting belief you have about money.
    - Ask: "Is this absolutely true?"
    - Replace with empowering alternatives like:
        - "Money supports my freedom."
        - "There's more than enough to go around."
2. *Feel Rich Before You Are*
    - Abundance isn't about having a million dollars. It's about feeling expansive.
    - Notice moments of overflow already in your life:
        - A delicious meal
        - A warm home
        - A genuine smile
    - Gratitude for what you already have expands your receiving energy.
3. *Normalize Money in Your Mind*
    - Visualize yourself confidently receiving, spending, investing, and donating money.
    - Don't worship money. Make it neutral, natural, and manageable in your imagination.
4. *Detach from the 'How'*
    - Don't limit the ways money can come to you.
    - Stay open to unexpected income, gifts, ideas, opportunities.

Daily Money Manifestation Practices

Affirmations:

- "I am open to receiving unlimited wealth."
- "Money flows to me from known and unknown sources."
- "I am a magnet for financial miracles."

Future Spending Lists:

- Write out what you'd joyfully spend money on if you had unlimited funds.
- Feel the excitement, ease, and generosity.

Wealth Anchoring:

- Carry a crisp $100 bill. Don't spend it, just know you *could*.
- This simple practice shifts your mindset from lack to possibility.

What to Avoid

> *Forcing or obsessing*: Obsession equals desperation, which sends a frequency of lack.

> *Fearful spending*: Every time you spend with fear, you reinforce scarcity. Spend with trust and gratitude.

> *Comparing your financial timeline*: Someone else's success has nothing to do with your path.

Receiving Is an Energy

Money responds to your ability to receive.
That includes:

- ➤ Accepting compliments
- ➤ Asking for help
- ➤ Charging fairly for your time or work
- ➤ Saying "yes" to opportunities that stretch you

When you say "I'm ready," the Universe listens, but only if your energy supports your words.

Manifesting money isn't about greed or materialism. It's about stepping into your natural state of flow, security, and creative expression.

Wealth is just one form of energy and you're meant to let it in, not chase it down.

When you shift from scarcity to sufficiency, money becomes a partner, not a problem.

Manifesting Career and Purpose

Creating work that lights you up and aligns with who you truly are.

One of the most fulfilling forms of manifestation is when you begin to live your purpose. It's when your work, passion, and personal values align into something that not only supports you, but inspires you.

But many people stay stuck in jobs or careers that feel draining, because they've been conditioned to believe:

> ➤ "Work has to be hard."
> ➤ "I can't make money doing what I love."
> ➤ "I don't know what my purpose is."

Manifestation turns that narrative upside down. It starts with the belief that your purpose already exists, and is trying to find you, too.

What Is Purpose, Really?

Purpose doesn't always mean a big, world-changing mission. Sometimes, it's:

- ➤ A quiet passion that energizes you.

- ➤ A role that uses your natural talents.

- ➤ A way you help others by just being yourself.

Purpose is less about what you *do* and more about how aligned you feel while doing it.

Aligning with a Fulfilling Career Path

1. *Clarity First*
   - Ask:
     - "What would I do if I didn't need money?"
     - "What activities make me lose track of time?"
     - "What do people always thank me for?"
   - The answers hold clues to your inner compass.
2. *Visualize Your Ideal Workday*
   - Forget job titles, focus on feelings.
   - Where are you?
   - Who are you working with?
   - What kind of problems are you solving?

Create a clear, vivid mental picture of your *energy at work.* Then align your current habits to that future self.

3. *Follow the Pull, Not the Pressure*
   - Inspired action means taking steps that feel exciting or intriguing, even if they don't make total sense yet.
   - That could mean starting a blog, networking with someone in your dream industry, or learning a new skill.
   - The Universe needs your movement to match your intention.

Manifestation Mistakes in Career Pursuits

> *Waiting for permission:* Stop waiting to be "qualified" or "ready." Confidence comes after you begin.

> *Focusing only on money:* If the only goal is a paycheck, fulfillment may never follow.

> *Ignoring joy:* Joy is guidance. If a path makes you feel alive, it's worth exploring.

Affirmations for Career and Purpose

- ➤ "I do meaningful work that aligns with my gifts."

- ➤ "My career grows effortlessly and supports my dream life."

- ➤ "I am always in the right place at the right time for new opportunities."

- ➤ "My purpose unfolds naturally, step by step."

Trusting the Unfolding

You may not see the full picture now, and that's okay.

Careers and callings evolve. What matters is that you stay open to nudges, pay attention to excitement, and trust that *your path will become clear the more you walk it.*

If you're stuck, start anywhere. Begin with what lights you up, and the next step will find you.

Manifesting Health and Vitality

Aligning body, mind, and energy for true wellness.

Health is the foundation of everything else you want to experience: love, abundance, purpose. Without energy, clarity, and physical well-being, manifestation becomes an uphill climb. But here's the powerful truth:

Your body responds to your thoughts, emotions, and energy.
Healing isn't just physical, it's energetic alignment in motion.

While it's not about ignoring real medical care, manifesting health works alongside it by creating an internal environment that supports healing, vitality, and wholeness.

Your Body Hears Everything You Think

Your cells are listening.

> ➤ When you think, *"I'm always tired,"* your body complies.

> ➤ When you affirm, *"I'm getting stronger and healthier every day,"* your body begins adjusting to match.

Every thought you have is like an instruction to your body. The question is: are you giving empowering instructions or harmful ones?

Steps to Manifest Better Health

1. *Change Your Health Story*
   - Let go of identity statements like:
     - "I have a weak immune system."
     - "I'm just not athletic."
   - Replace with:
     - "My body is healing more every day."
     - "I trust my body's wisdom."
2. *Visualize a Vibrant You*
   - Don't just think "I want to be healthy."
   - Imagine yourself full of energy, smiling, moving freely, sleeping deeply, glowing.
   - Engage your senses: What do you see, feel, hear when you're at peak vitality?
3. *Listen to the Signals, Not Just the Symptoms*
   - Fatigue, pain, or cravings often have emotional or energetic roots.
   - Ask your body: *"What are you trying to tell me?"*
   - Journaling, meditation, or even gentle movement can help decode the message.
4. *Raise Your Vibration with Nourishment*
   - Food, water, sleep, and movement aren't just survival needs - they're energy conductors.
   - Choose what fuels vitality, not what numbs it.

The Emotional-Health Connection

Emotions like resentment, fear, and guilt can create energetic blocks in the body.
Releasing those emotions (through shadow work, forgiveness, or inner healing) can lead to physical relief.

Don't underestimate the power of:

- Laughing often

- Crying when needed

- Breathing deeply

- Practicing gratitude for your body, even in imperfection

Affirmations for Health and Vitality

> ➤ "My body knows how to heal and thrive."

> ➤ "Every cell in my body is filled with light and strength."

> ➤ "I treat my body with kindness and respect."

> ➤ "Health is my natural state."

Your health manifestation is not a fight, it's a return to balance.

By shifting your thoughts, honoring your body's messages, and aligning your energy with vitality, you allow your natural state of well-being to rise to the surface.

Your body wants to thrive. You just have to give it the permission and the belief.

Chapter 9: Unique and Modern Approaches

- Using AI as a Manifestation Support Tool (vision board generation, journaling, affirmations)
- Reality Shifting vs. Manifestation: What's the Difference?
- Using Music, Art, and Creativity to Manifest

Using AI as a Manifestation Support Tool

Leveraging technology to amplify clarity, consistency, and creativity.

In today's world, the tools we use to manifest don't have to be limited to notebooks, mood boards, or silent meditation. Artificial Intelligence (AI) can now be a powerful, practical ally in your manifestation journey.

Used with the right mindset, AI becomes more than just a gadget - it becomes a mirror, a motivator, and a creative partner.

Why Use AI for Manifestation?

➤ *Speed:* AI helps you clarify goals faster than your own overthinking mind might allow.

➤ *Structure:* It brings order to scattered thoughts through organized journaling and task-setting.

➤ *Inspiration:* AI can generate ideas, prompts, and visuals that spark your imagination in new directions.

The key? *You remain the conscious creator.*
AI is just the amplifier of your focus.

1. Vision Board Generation with AI Tools

You no longer need scissors and magazines to make a vision board.

> ➤ AI-powered design tools can create digital visuals of your dream life.

> ➤ Want to see yourself in your dream home? Wearing your ideal outfit? Standing in front of your future business? AI can now create photo-realistic images that reflect your desired reality.

Why it works:
When you see yourself in that reality, even as a digital image, your subconscious starts to normalize that version of you.

2. Journaling and Prompting with AI

Manifestation journaling can be hard when you don't know what to write. AI journaling assistants (like ChatGPT) can:

> Generate reflection prompts based on your goals.

> Help reframe limiting beliefs into affirmations.

> Track themes or progress in your daily thoughts.

Try this prompt:
"Give me 5 journaling questions to align with abundance today."
or
"Help me write a script for my ideal morning as if I'm already living it."

3. Affirmation Support

AI can:

> ➢ Personalize affirmations based on your emotional state.

> ➢ Help reword affirmations that feel forced or fake.

> ➢ Deliver affirmations in your voice using text-to-speech tools for audio repetition.

This transforms affirmations from robotic phrases into emotionally resonant statements that actually stick.

4. Habit & Focus Trackers with AI Integration

Apps like Notion, Habitica, or even wearable tech integrated with AI can help you:

- ➢ Track daily manifestation rituals (like visualizing, meditating, or scripting).

- ➢ Spot patterns in your energy and mindset over time.

- ➢ Gamify consistency, because repetition builds belief.

Important Reminder

AI is powerful, but it doesn't replace your inner alignment.

You still need:

> ➤ Clarity: Know what you want.

> ➤ Belief: Trust you're worthy of it.

> ➤ Action: Stay open and responsive to intuitive nudges.

AI is the assistant. You're the architect.

Using AI in your manifestation process isn't about becoming robotic, it's about using smart tools to free up more space for feeling, envisioning, and creating.

When your tech is aligned with your intention, it becomes a sacred tool, not just a screen.

Reality Shifting vs. Manifestation: What's the Difference?

Exploring two paths to creating your ideal reality, and when to use each.

In the online space, especially among younger audiences, "reality shifting" has gained massive attention alongside manifestation. While they share some similarities, they're not the same thing, and understanding the difference helps you use both with clarity.

Let's break it down in the simplest way possible.

Manifestation: Shaping Your Current Reality

Definition: Manifestation is the process of attracting experiences, people, and opportunities into your current timeline by aligning your thoughts, emotions, and beliefs with what you want.

In simple terms:
You stay in this world, but make it better by changing yourself.

You manifest by:

> *Getting clear on what you desire.*
> *Believing it's possible and that you're worthy.*
> *Taking inspired actions.*
> *Trusting the outcome.*

Key traits:

> *Grounded in this 3D reality.*
> *Focused on growth, healing, and alignment.*
> *Works with time - progressive unfolding.*

Reality Shifting: Choosing a New Timeline or Dimension

Definition: Reality shifting is the idea that you can move your consciousness into a different version of reality - whether that's a fictional world, an alternate universe, or a different timeline where your desires already exist.

In simple terms:
You shift to a parallel version of reality that already holds what you want.

Popularized in online communities like TikTok and Reddit, people often use shifting to visit fictional realities (like Hogwarts or other imagined places), but the deeper principle is this:

You are the observer.
And the observer can shift focus, and shift dimensions.

Key traits:

> *More metaphysical and quantum-based.*
> *Involves altered states (meditation, sleep, deep focus).*
> *Often includes scripting and pre-planned "Desired Realities" (DRs).*
> *May involve temporary or permanent shifts in perception.*

How Are They Similar?

- ➢ Both rely on belief, focus, and emotion.
- ➢ Both suggest reality is not fixed. It bends based on your consciousness.
- ➢ Both involve scripting, visualization, and inner alignment.
- ➢ Both empower you to stop being a passive victim and become a conscious creator.

How Are They Different?

Manifestation	Reality Shifting
Alters current life through alignment	Moves awareness to another version
Involves physical action and time	Can feel instant or surreal
More grounded in psychology + energy	More rooted in quantum/multiverse theory
Focuses on attracting outcomes	Focuses on entering a different reality
Long-term lifestyle tool	Often seen as temporary or specific

Which One Is "Better"?

Neither is better - just different tools for different intentions.

> ➤ Want to grow your business, attract a partner, or heal emotionally?
>   → Manifestation is your grounded go-to.
> ➤ Want to explore alternate realities, boost creativity, or experience radical detachment from limitations?
>   → Shifting might open doors you didn't even know existed.

Some people use both:

> ➤ Manifest in daily life, and
> ➤ Shift for creativity, healing, or alternate exploration.

Manifestation is about becoming a magnet.
Reality shifting is about becoming a traveler.

Both remind you: Reality is flexible, and you are more powerful than you've been taught.

Using Music, Art, and Creativity to Manifest

How self-expression becomes a channel for transformation.

Most people think of manifestation as mental: think it, believe it, attract it.

But manifestation isn't just a mind game - it's an energetic act, and few things shift energy faster than creativity.

Whether it's music, painting, dance, or writing, engaging with creativity puts you into a state of flow, where resistance drops, joy rises, and alignment happens naturally.

Why Creativity Supercharges Manifestation

1. *Emotion = Energy in Motion*
   Creative acts are rich with emotion.
   And in manifestation, feeling is everything.

   - A love song can lift your vibration.
   - A painting can hold the vision of your dream home.
   - A poem can lock in your belief like an affirmation.

2. *Bypassing the Critical Mind*
   When you're singing, doodling, or dancing, you stop overthinking.
   That's when the subconscious opens and your desires slip in easier.

3. *Creating Mirrors Reality Creation*
   When you paint, write, or produce music, you're practicing creation.
   That's the same muscle you use to manifest your life.

Every time you make something from nothing, you're rehearsing the act of creation itself.

Ways to Use Music, Art, and Creativity in Manifestation

1. Musical Anchors

> ➤ *Create playlists that match the* vibe *of what you're calling in.*
> ➤ *Listen while journaling, visualizing, or exercising.*
> ➤ *Associate each playlist with a manifestation (love, abundance, healing).*

Music helps entrain your nervous system to a new frequency. Over time, your body begins to *feel* what it's like to already have what you want.

2. Manifestation Art

> ➤ Paint or draw symbols, environments, or abstract forms that represent your desires.
> ➤ No need to be an artist. This is about energy, not skill.
> ➤ Place your creations where you'll see them daily. This becomes a vibrational reminder.

3. Dance and Movement

> ➢ Movement is manifestation in motion.
> ➢ Put on a song that matches the life you want, and dance *as if* you're already living it.
> ➢ Bonus: This helps release blocks stuck in the body.

4. Creative Scripting

> ➢ Write your goals as poetry, song lyrics, or even short stories.
> ➢ Imagine a day in your dream life and write it like a movie scene.
> ➢ This engages imagination *and* emotion - two manifestation power tools.

Creativity Is Not a Hobby. It's a Frequency

The more you create, the more you embody creation itself.
This shifts you out of passivity and into power.

Even small creative rituals (like 5 minutes of humming, sketching, or journaling) can center you, lift you, and move you closer to your desires.

Creativity Helps You

You don't need a perfect vision board or flawless affirmations.

Sometimes, your breakthrough comes when you:

- ➢ Scribble in a journal.

- ➢ Sing in the shower.

- ➢ Dance in your room.

- ➢ Write a love song to your future self.

Creativity is manifestation with color.
And when you let your soul express, the universe responds in kind.

Chapter 10: Real Stories, Real Results

- Reader/Client Testimonials or Case Studies
- "This Worked for Me" Personal Account

Reader/Client Testimonials or Case Studies

Proof that this works: from real people, just like you.

Theory is powerful. But nothing builds trust and belief like seeing real lives transformed. These stories aren't from celebrities or gurus - they're from everyday people who decided to apply the techniques you've read about in this book.

Each case study reveals how simple practices, when done with consistency and intention, can lead to real, tangible results - often faster than expected.

Case Study #1: From Overwhelmed to Overflowing

<u>Name</u>: Maya, 34; Freelance Graphic Designer
<u>Manifestation Focus</u>: Financial stability and consistent clients
<u>Main Technique Used</u>: Scripting + AI-generated vision boards

<u>Before:</u>
Maya struggled with feast-or-famine income cycles. She would land a few gigs, then fall into a dry spell that lasted months. She doubted whether she could continue freelancing full-time.

<u>What Changed:</u>
She began scripting her ideal day every morning as if she already had her dream clients.
She also used AI to generate a vision board that showed her working from cafes, collaborating with brands, and living comfortably.

<u>Results (in 6 weeks):</u>

- ➢ Signed two long-term clients
- ➢ Paid off a major credit card
- ➢ Reported feeling more confident and "less needy" in client calls

"Seeing my vision board made it feel like that life already belonged to me. Once I believed that, the work started showing up."

Case Study #2: A New Reality in Love

<u>Name</u>: Jordan, 27; Customer Service Rep
<u>Manifestation Focus</u>: Attracting a conscious relationship
<u>Main Technique Used</u>: The "Wouldn't It Be Nice If..."

<u>Before</u>:
Jordan had been single for three years and kept attracting emotionally unavailable partners. He was starting to believe he'd never meet someone who truly "got" him.

<u>What Changed</u>:
He began using the "Wouldn't It Be Nice If..." technique every evening and allowed himself to feel the warmth of being in a relationship. He didn't force it.He just gently aligned with the possibility.

<u>Results (in 2 months)</u>:

- ➢ Met someone through a friend of a friend
- ➢ Relationship began organically and progressed with ease
- ➢ Reported feeling "seen and valued" in ways he hadn't before

"I wasn't desperate anymore. I was curious. That changed everything."

Case Study #3: The Inner Block That Opened the Door

Name: Selene, 41; Stay-at-home mom turned entrepreneur
Manifestation Focus: Launching her first product
Main Technique Used: Shadow work + Quantum Shift Meditation

Before:
Selene had a dream of selling handmade skincare but kept self-sabotaging. She felt like a fraud, worried people wouldn't take her seriously.

What Changed:
She worked through limiting beliefs around "not being business-minded" and began forgiving herself for past failures. Then, she did the Quantum Shift Meditation three times a week to embody her successful self.

Results (in 3 months):

- ➤ Launched an online shop
- ➤ Made her first 50 sales
- ➤ Got featured by a local influencer
- ➤ Now sees herself as a "creative businesswoman," not "just a mom"

"It wasn't about the products. It was about who I believed I could become."

The common thread in every story

They started before they felt ready.

They chose belief, practiced daily, and took inspired steps.

These are real people. If it worked for them, it can absolutely work for you.

"This Worked for Me" - Personal Account

A candid reflection from the author on what truly made the difference.

When I first heard about manifestation, I was intrigued but skeptical. The idea that thoughts could shape reality sounded beautiful, but unrealistic. I believed in hard work, logic, and strategy. Magic? That felt like a fantasy.

But everything changed when I hit a wall in my own life.

I had dreams, but they weren't happening. I was doing "all the right things," yet nothing moved. I was tired, stuck, and disconnected.

So I gave manifestation a shot. Not in a "vision board and wishful thinking" way, but in a grounded, curious way. I approached it like an experiment. If it works, great. If not, no harm done.

I will share with you what genuinely worked for me.

1. Deciding Was More Powerful Than Wanting

The shift from *"I hope I get this…"* to *"This is happening, I'm choosing it"* changed everything.

I stopped begging the universe. I started collaborating with it.

When I decided I was no longer available for certain patterns - like financial stress or low self-worth - things started rearranging. Fast.

2. Emotion Was the Secret Sauce

For months I said affirmations with my head, but nothing changed.

Then I learned to feel them.

I'd visualize my dream life and let my body respond: goosebumps, tears, laughter, joy. That emotion gave the words power. That's when I started seeing results.

3. Small Habits Had Big Results

I didn't need to meditate for an hour or journal for 12 pages. What worked was:

> ➤ 2-minute micro-affirmations in the mirror
> ➤ 5-minute visualizations before sleep
> ➤ One line of scripting a day

Small, consistent signals to the universe that said: *"This is who I am becoming."*

4. Shadow Work Was the Key That Unlocked It All

I couldn't manifest past my inner resistance.

It wasn't that the universe was ignoring me - it's that I wasn't letting it in.

Once I started facing my fears, insecurities, and buried stories (gently, not harshly), things started flowing with less effort.

5. The Best Results Came When I Let Go

My biggest breakthroughs always came after I stopped obsessing.
I did the work, trusted it was in motion, and got back to living.

That's when the email arrived, the offer came, or the opportunity
showed up "out of nowhere."
Only it wasn't out of nowhere. It was the result of alignment.

I'm not here to convince you.
I'm here to say: *This worked for me. Maybe it will for you, too.*

And if you approach it with open-hearted curiosity and commitment
(not perfection), you might just surprise yourself.

This is your life.
You're not just living it.
You're creating it.

Chapter 11: Troubleshooting: When It's Not Working

- What to Do When You Feel Stuck
- How to Manifest During Anxiety or Depression
- Releasing Timelines and Doubts

What to Do When You Feel Stuck

Because even the most aligned creators hit a wall sometimes.

Manifestation isn't always a smooth, magical flow. Sometimes, it feels like shouting into the void. You do the visualizations. You write the affirmations. You take inspired action. And still… nothing.

So, what do you do when you feel stuck?

The answer isn't to push harder - it's to shift the energy.

First, Stop Blaming Yourself

Getting stuck doesn't mean you're broken or doing it wrong. It's part of the process.

Sometimes, stuckness is the universe's way of saying: *"There's something deeper here. Let's look at it together."*

Approach yourself with compassion, not criticism.

Zoom Out and Reconnect to the Why

When you're too deep in the "how" and "when," you lose sight of the "why."

Ask yourself:

> ➢ *Why do I want this?*
> ➢ *How will this desire make me feel?*
> ➢ *Who am I becoming through this journey?*

Reconnecting with your purpose reignites energy. It transforms the goal from a pressure point into an inspiring pull.

Do an Energetic Reset

Stuck energy often calls for a pattern interrupt. Try:

> ➢ Decluttering your space
> ➢ Changing your daily routine
> ➢ Spending a day without trying to manifest anything
> ➢ Going on a walk without your phone

The smallest reset in your external world can jolt your inner world back into flow.

Look for Hidden Resistance

Ask yourself gently:

> ➢ *Am I secretly afraid of getting what I want?*
> ➢ *Is there a belief saying I don't deserve it?*
> ➢ *Do I think it has to be hard to be real?*

This isn't about judgment. It's about awareness. Once you see the resistance, you can start to dissolve it.

Try a New Technique

Sometimes, you're not stuck. You're just bored.
Your mind and body crave freshness. Try:

> ➢ A new scripting format (e.g., future diary)
> ➢ A visualization with music and movement
> ➢ Manifestation with art, painting, or dance
> ➢ Writing a "letter from your future self"

Novelty rekindles excitement. And excitement is fuel for creation.

Take a Break From "Trying"

There's power in detachment.
When you rest, play, and enjoy your life as it is, you become
magnetic. It's not giving up. It's letting go of *needing* it to happen
right now.

Manifestation flows best through openness, not pressure.

Feeling stuck isn't failure.
It's feedback.
And often, it's the pause before the leap forward.

The energy will move again. It always does. Your job is to stay
connected to your vision, and keep your heart open.

How to Manifest During Anxiety or Depression

Because manifestation isn't just for your high-vibe days.

One of the most common misconceptions is that you have to be happy, high-vibe, and radiating joy 24/7 in order to manifest anything. But what about the days when you're anxious, low, or deep in depression?

The truth is: you can still manifest, even during emotional struggle. But the approach needs to be softer, more compassionate, and rooted in self-care.

Start Where You Are, Not Where You Think You Should Be

Don't fake positivity. Don't force high vibrations.
Instead, meet yourself where you are - with honesty and grace.

If you're sad, anxious, or overwhelmed, acknowledge it. Say:

"This is how I feel right now, and it's okay. I can still choose to create something new."

This small act of self-acceptance is a manifestation in itself: it shifts your inner frequency from resistance to presence.

Shift from Big Goals to Gentle Intentions

During hard times, the idea of manifesting a dream job or soulmate can feel far away. That's okay.

Instead, focus on tiny, soothing intentions, like:

> ➤ "I want to feel a little more peace today."
> ➤ "I want to notice something beautiful."
> ➤ "I'd love for one kind moment to find me."

These micro-intentions are powerful. They build emotional momentum and restore your belief one gentle moment at a time.

Focus on Nourishing, Not Fixing

When anxious or depressed, avoid "fixing" yourself through manifestation.
Instead, use it to nourish your spirit. Ask:

> ➤ What would make me feel safe right now?
> ➤ What thought feels like a warm blanket?
> ➤ What's the most loving next step I can take?

Your emotional healing is not separate from your manifestation journey.
It *is* the journey.

Use Grounding Techniques That Anchor You

Your nervous system is part of the equation.
Grounding tools can help regulate your energy and open you up to
receive, even if just slightly:

- ➢ Slow, deep breaths (in through nose, out through mouth)
- ➢ Warm showers with visualization
- ➢ Journaling your feelings without judgment
- ➢ Putting your bare feet on the earth
- ➢ Listening to calming music or frequencies

When your body feels safe, your heart can open again.

Trust That Healing *Is* Manifestation

You're not off-track because you're not manifesting "big things."
If you're choosing to rest, seek help, feel your feelings, or even just
breathe through a tough moment, you are manifesting healing,
resilience, and inner strength.

Those things matter just as much (if not more) than anything
external.

Reminder

You are not behind. You are not broken. You are not blocked.
You are growing, even if it's beneath the surface right now.
Even in your darkest days, the universe hears your whisper.

So take it slow.
Feel what you feel.
And know that your dreams still belong to you - even here.

Releasing Timelines and Doubts

Because needing it now often pushes it further away.

One of the most frustrating parts of manifestation is the waiting.

You've set your intention, done the inner work, taken action. And still, the result isn't here. Days turn into weeks, weeks into months. And doubt starts to creep in.

This is where many people unknowingly slow down or block their manifestations - not because they're doing it wrong, but because they're clinging too tightly to *when* and *how*.

Let's unpack why timelines and doubts are normal, and how to release their grip.

1. Timelines Are Mental, Not Universal

Your mind creates a timeline based on logic, urgency, or comparison.
But the universe doesn't follow your clock. It operates on alignment, not deadlines.

Sometimes what you want is ready.
Sometimes *you're* being readied for it.

Either way, trust that the delay is not a denial, but a divine recalibration.

2. Doubt Doesn't Cancel Your Manifestation

Everyone doubts. You're human.

Doubt only becomes a problem when you let it build a narrative:

> "Maybe I'm not good enough."
> "Maybe it's not meant for me."
> "I must be doing it wrong."

Instead of wrestling doubt, observe it.
Say: *"I notice this doubt, but I choose to believe anyway."*
Faith is not the absence of doubt, it's the decision to move with trust despite it.

3. Practice Emotional Detachment (Not Indifference)

Detachment doesn't mean you stop caring. It means you stop obsessing.

When you let go of *needing* it to happen a certain way or by a certain date, you:

> Create emotional space for it to arrive
> Stay present and open to different (often better) paths
> Regain your peace and joy *now*, not "someday"

This doesn't weaken your manifestation - it strengthens your receiving channel.

4. Use the "It's Already Done" Mindset

Instead of asking *"When will it come?"*, try:

> ➢ "It's already on its way."
> ➢ "I trust the timing is being worked out."
> ➢ "The universe is aligning everything in my favor."

This mindset shift calms your nervous system, raises your vibration, and magnetizes aligned action.

5. Turn Waiting Into Living

Don't put your life on pause while waiting for a manifestation.

Instead of checking the mailbox or refreshing your bank app 10 times a day, ask:

> ➢ *What brings me joy today?*
> ➢ *How can I love this current chapter more fully?*
> ➢ *What can I give, learn, or create now?*

Paradoxically, the more you live, the faster things flow.

So, Just Remember

Letting go of timelines doesn't mean giving up, it means handing over the stopwatch and trusting divine timing.

When you stop staring at the clock, you hear more guidance.
When you release the doubt, you make room for miracles.

It's coming.
Just maybe not on the day you circled on your calendar.

Chapter 12: Creating Your Personal Manifestation Blueprint

- Designing a Manifestation Plan That Suits Your Lifestyle
- Mixing and Matching Techniques
- Tracking and Celebrating Progress

Designing a Manifestation Plan That Suits Your Lifestyle

Because there's no one-size-fits-all method, and there shouldn't be.

One of the most empowering truths about manifestation is this: You get to do it your way.
No rulebook. No rigid steps. No pressure to copy someone else's process.

Instead of trying to fit your life around a manifestation method, let's design a blueprint that naturally fits *you*: your energy, your rhythm, your schedule, and your personality.

Let's see how.

1. Know Your Manifestation Style

Are you *a visual thinker? A writer? A feeler? A doer?*

Some people connect best through:

- ➢ Visualization and vision boards

- ➢ Journaling and scripting

- ➢ Speaking affirmations aloud

- ➢ Moving their body or creating art

- ➢ Silent meditation or walking in nature

Pay attention to what feels most natural and exciting.
Your blueprint starts with what already works *for you.*

2. Consider Your Schedule and Energy Levels

You don't need a 2-hour morning routine to manifest.
You don't need to meditate like a monk.
You just need *consistency in a form that feels doable.*

Ask yourself:

> ➤ When do I feel most clear or inspired - morning, midday, or night?
> ➤ Do I prefer short, frequent practices or one longer weekly session?
> ➤ What can I realistically commit to every day or week?

Examples:

> ➤ 5-minute visualization during coffee
> ➤ 3 affirmations in the mirror before leaving the house
> ➤ Journaling 2x a week before bed
> ➤ One deep focus session every Sunday

Even 5 minutes, done with presence, can shift your reality.

3. Choose Your Core Practices

Think of these as the pillars of your plan. Choose 2–3 main techniques that feel aligned and manageable. For example:

> ➤ Morning affirmations

> ➤ Weekly scripting

> ➤ Occasional two-cup method

> ➤ Monthly visualization refresh

You don't need to use *every* method from this book.
Pick the ones that *click*. Leave the rest. This is your plan.

4. Set a Gentle Structure, Not a Strict Routine

Structure creates momentum, but rigidity kills joy.
Instead of saying "I *have* to do XYZ daily," try:

> ➤ "I *get* to do these practices when I feel drawn."

> ➤ "I'll check in with myself each morning and choose what I need."

> ➤ "These are the tools in my toolbox, I'll use them as needed."

Give yourself permission to adapt. Your life changes. So will your plan.

5. Make It Sacred, Not Just Productive

Your manifestation blueprint isn't a chore list.
It's a sacred space where you:

- ➤ Remember your power

- ➤ Align with your truth

- ➤ Receive intuitive guidance

- ➤ Activate your creative role in the universe

So light a candle, play soft music, go barefoot, sip tea - whatever makes it feel magical and nourishing.

This is your manifestation sanctuary.

Choose What's More Suitable for You

The best manifestation plan is the one you actually use - because it feels *good*, *sustainable*, and *personal*.

Your life is unique. Your path will be too.

You don't need more pressure. You need permission.

To manifest your dream life, design a plan that already fits into the one you have.

Mixing and Matching Techniques

Because you're allowed to blend, remix, and evolve your way to success.

Manifestation isn't about choosing one technique and sticking to it forever. It's about building a custom toolkit that reflects your evolving desires, moods, and growth.

Just like a workout routine or skincare regimen, mixing and matching creates balance and keeps the process fresh and fun.

Let's see how to become your own manifestation "alchemist."

1. Understand the Strengths of Each Technique

Different manifestation methods activate different parts of your mind and energy field.

For example:

> ➤ Visualization activates imagination and emotional vibration

> ➤ Scripting connects your logical mind with subconscious belief

> ➤ Affirmations rewire habitual thoughts and self-talk

> ➤ Meditation clears resistance and opens receiving channels

> ➤ The Two-Cup Method works on symbolic and subconscious levels

> ➤ Micro-affirmations or "Wouldn't it be nice if…" create soft, daily momentum

By understanding what each tool *does*, you can combine them more intentionally.

2. Create Layered Routines (Without Overcomplicating)

You can "stack" techniques into brief, daily rituals. For example:

Morning Boost Routine (10 min)

> ➤ *Say 3 affirmations in the mirror*
> ➤ *Visualize one goal for 2 minutes*
> ➤ *Write a quick "Wouldn't it be nice if..." statement*

Weekly Manifestation Session (20–30 min)

> ➤ Journal or script a future diary entry
> ➤ Use a guided meditation or quantum shift visualization
> ➤ Update your vision board or reflect on progress

Blending a few techniques at a time keeps things dynamic and powerful.

3. Adjust Based on Mood and Energy

Feeling energized? Go deep with scripting or meditation.
Feeling scattered or tired? Try a one-liner affirmation or gentle walk with intention.

The key is to match the technique to your state. This honors your flow and prevents burnout.

Your plan should support you, not stress you.

4. Know When to Switch It Up

Sometimes, a technique stops resonating, and that's okay.

Signs it's time to try something new:

- ➢ You're going through the motions without feeling it
- ➢ It starts to feel like a task, not a tool
- ➢ You're curious about something different

Don't see this as failure. See it as evolution.
Growth naturally brings new tools into your awareness.

5. Combine Modern Tools with Ancient Wisdom

You can even mix modern approaches with spiritual or traditional ones.

Example blends:

> ➢ Use AI to generate vision board images, then meditate on them

> ➢ Write affirmations with a digital journal and add emojis or art

> ➢ Record your affirmations and listen back as a voice memo

> ➢ Do a quantum shift meditation while holding a symbolic object or crystal

There are no rules - just resonance.

Be Flexible

Mixing and matching techniques is how you take *ownership* of your practice.

It's where manifestation becomes not just effective, but enjoyable, personal, and alive.

This is where you stop being a follower and become a creator of your own process.

Keep what works. Try what excites. Drop what drains.

Build a toolkit that grows with you.

Tracking and Celebrating Progress

Because every small win is a sign your manifestation is working - even before the big results show up.

Most people miss their manifestations not because they're not happening, but because they're not *noticing* them.

That's where tracking and celebrating come in. These habits keep you focused, grateful, and in energetic alignment with even more good things.

Let's break it down.

1. Why Tracking Matters

Tracking is not about obsessing.
It's about staying *aware*. Noticing what's shifting. Honoring the signs. Building confidence.

Benefits of tracking your manifestation journey:

> ➤ Shows evidence that it's working
> ➤ Reinforces belief and momentum
> ➤ Helps spot patterns (what works best for you?)
> ➤ Keeps your goals top-of-mind without pressure

Even tiny synchronicities or mood shifts count as progress.
Document those too.

2. What to Track

Here are things you can start tracking:

- ➤ *Synchronicities and "signs" (e.g., repeating numbers, unexpected opportunities)*
- ➤ *Mood or energy improvements*
- ➤ *Mini-wins or manifestations (even if they're small)*
- ➤ *Intuitive nudges you followed*
- ➤ *Completed practices (visualization, scripting, etc.)*

You can use:

- ➤ *A journal*
- ➤ *A manifestation app*
- ➤ *A calendar*
- ➤ *Sticky notes on your mirror*
- ➤ *Voice memos*
  Pick what's easy and fun for you.

3. Celebrate Small Wins (Like They're Big)

The universe loves appreciation.
When you celebrate, you amplify your vibration and attract more to celebrate.

Examples of things worth celebrating:

- ➢ You stayed consistent for a week
- ➢ You noticed a repeating number
- ➢ You felt emotionally aligned all day
- ➢ You manifested a free coffee or a helpful message

It doesn't have to be the *final goal* to be worth noticing. Every win is a sign the path is unfolding.

Ways to celebrate:

- ➢ Say "thank you" out loud
- ➢ Write it in your journal in bold letters
- ➢ Do a happy dance
- ➢ Treat yourself to something small and joyful

4. Progress Isn't Always Linear

Some days you'll feel unstoppable. Others, not so much.

That's normal.

Tracking and celebrating keep you grounded *through both*.
You'll start to see that even on off-days, progress is happening beneath the surface.

Trust in the process. It deepens with time, and evidence.

Honor Your Progress

Progress is the invisible thread that connects intention to reality.
By noticing and honoring it (no matter how subtle), you stay aligned,
empowered, and ready to receive more.

You are manifesting *right now.*
You're already on your way.
Celebrate that.

Chapter 13: Conclusion & Next Steps

- How to Stay Consistent Without Obsessing
- Final Words of Encouragement

How to Stay Consistent Without Obsessing

Because manifestation should be a lifestyle, not a full-time job.

One of the biggest challenges in manifestation is walking the fine line between staying focused and relaxed.

You want to be intentional, but not clingy.
You want to stay in alignment, but not obsess over every detail.

So how do you stay consistent without turning it into pressure or perfectionism?

1. Think in Terms of Ritual, Not Routine

Routines can start to feel robotic.
Rituals, on the other hand, are sacred, intentional moments you get to enjoy.

Instead of thinking, "Ugh, I *have to* visualize,"
Think: "I *get to* spend 5 minutes seeing my dream life."

Make it feel good. Light a candle. Play calming music. Say your affirmations in the mirror with a smile.
The more you *enjoy* the process, the easier it is to show up for it.

2. Less Time, More Impact

You don't need to spend an hour a day manifesting.
In fact, micro moments can be just as powerful when done with
focus.

Try:

- ➤ A 17-second burst of focused thought
- ➤ Whispering an affirmation while making coffee
- ➤ Gratitude journaling while winding down at night
- ➤ Using a lock screen image as a daily visual reminder

Small, consistent touches keep your energy in alignment without
burnout.

3. Use Triggers and Anchors

Pair your manifestation practices with daily habits to make them automatic. For example:

➤ Say your affirmations right after brushing your teeth
➤ Do a 2-minute visualization during your commute
➤ Reflect on a win from your day while lying in bed

This builds consistency with *zero extra effort* - because your brain loves patterns.

4. Detachment is Part of the Process

Here's the truth: trying *too* hard can actually slow things down.

When you cling, worry, or keep checking for results, you signal to your subconscious that you don't yet believe.

Instead:

➤ Do your part
➤ Feel the feelings
➤ Then shift your focus and go live your life

Let it *marinate*. Trust the oven. Don't keep opening the door to check.

5. Create Check-In Points, Not Pressure

Rather than tracking every single day, try weekly or bi-weekly check-ins:

> ➢ "How am I feeling about my desires right now?"
> ➢ "What progress have I noticed?"
> ➢ "What technique do I feel drawn to this week?"

This allows flow and flexibility without slipping into obsession.

Consistency isn't about being perfect. It's about *showing up gently but often.*
Manifestation is a relationship with your future self. Keep it healthy, balanced, and joyful.

You don't have to force magic. Just keep making space for it.

Final Words of Encouragement

You are not starting from scratch. You are returning to your power.

If you've made it this far, it means you've already taken the most important step: you've chosen to believe that change is possible.

That quiet decision, even if uncertain at first, is the spark that ignites everything.

Your Desires Are Valid

You don't need to justify your dreams to anyone. Not even yourself.

The desire you feel wasn't placed in your heart randomly. It's a signal, a blueprint, a compass.

You were never meant to just survive. You were meant to create, expand, and experience joy.

You're Allowed to Take Up Space

So often, we dim our light thinking it's "too much" to want more love, more money, more fulfillment.

But abundance isn't selfish. Manifesting your dream life isn't greedy.
When you thrive, you become a living permission slip for others to do the same.

You Don't Have to Be Perfect to Manifest

Some days will feel magical. Other days, you'll doubt everything.

That's okay.

This isn't about perfect vibes or endless positivity. It's about showing up, even imperfectly, and trusting that the universe knows how to meet you halfway.

Trust the Timing, Trust Yourself

It might not all come at once, but that doesn't mean it's not coming.

Every aligned thought, every moment of clarity, every breath of gratitude - it all counts.
You're shaping reality in ways you may not even see yet.

Don't stop five minutes before the miracle.

Your Future is Already Waiting

You now have the tools, the mindset, and the awareness to create something extraordinary.
Whether you re-read this book, share it with someone else, or simply carry a piece of it in your heart,
Know this:

You are a powerful creator.
You always have been.

Now go create something beautiful.

The End.

(Unless it's just the beginning.)

Made in United States
Cleveland, OH
03 June 2025

17471699R10148